CEYLON

*An Introduction
to the "Resplendent Land"*

The Asia Library

THAILAND: An Introduction to Modern Siam
by NOEL F. BUSCH

CEYLON: An Introduction
to the "Resplendent Land"
by ARGUS JOHN TRESIDDER

CEYLON

An Introduction
to the "Resplendent Land"

by
ARGUS JOHN TRESIDDER

DRAWINGS BY NANCY PALMER TRESIDDER
MAP BY DOROTHY DE FONTAINE

D. VAN NOSTRAND COMPANY, INC.
PRINCETON, NEW JERSEY
Toronto · London · New York

D. VAN NOSTRAND COMPANY, INC.

120 Alexander St., Princeton, New Jersey (*Principal office*)
24 West 40 St., New York 18, New York

D. VAN NOSTRAND COMPANY, LTD.

358, Kensington High Street, London, W.14, England

D. VAN NOSTRAND COMPANY (Canada), LTD.

25 Hollinger Road, Toronto 16, Canada

Published simultaneously in Canada by
D. VAN NOSTRAND COMPANY (Canada), LTD.

Library of Congress Catalogue Card No. 60-9038

This book is one of the volumes in *The Asia Library,* a series initiated by The Asia Society, Inc., a non-profit, non-political, membership association whose purpose is to help bring the people of America and Asia closer together in their appreciation of each other and each other's way of life.

05602a30

PRINTED IN THE UNITED STATES OF AMERICA
BY LANCASTER PRESS, INC., LANCASTER, PA.

Preface

This little book is meant to be an *apéritif,* not an *entrée.* It should whet the appetite of those who hope to visit Ceylon or who may be stimulated to read about that delightful country in more comprehensive books. It is not a guide-book, though it may point the way to some of the most interesting and scenic places in the world; it is not a dissertation on the history, politics, economy, and culture of the country, though it may tell enough about those things to make the reader want to know more. In short, this book is aimed at those who know little about Ceylon. It is an introduction to Asia in miniature, to a country singularly favored by nature, the inheritor of noble traditions, the home of an ancient culture, the crossroads of the East. No book can ever do justice to the beauty and variety of Sri Lanka, the name which means the "resplendent land," but the story needs to be brought up to date.

There are many books about Ceylon, some of them written by big-game hunters, who were more interested in the leopards and pythons and elephants of Ceylon's jungles than in her history and culture, others by travelers or tea planters or economists, who empha- sized the scenery or the ruined cities or Ceylon's mountain-bound tea industry, or the enigma of a fertile country which prefers money-crops to food-crops and fails to grow enough food for its teeming population. The Ceylonese themselves have written well and proudly about their history and about their enduring arts. Yet this amiable country remains little known. Many Americans, for example, vaguely suppose that Ceylon is part of India and would have trouble in exactly locating it.

Since Sir Emerson Tennent wrote his definitive account of Ceylon a hundred years ago, many things have occurred that make a wider knowledge of this strategically located Asian country essential: Asia's important rubber industry was begun in Ceylon; a democratic society, a model to all Asia, was developed under the benevolent guidance of the British; the harbor at Trincomalee has been of potential value as a Free World naval base; Ceylon's position on principal ship and air routes has made it a popular site for major conferences, such as the Colombo Conference of 1950, many meetings of United Nations specialized organizations, some Communist-sponsored groups, and foundations and institutes interested in Asia; Ceylon has taken an increasingly active part in world affairs, notably at the Bandung Afro-Asian Conference in 1955 and in the United Nations report on the Hungarian rebellion against totalitarian domination in 1957. All thoughtful observers of the strains everywhere present in the modern world are watching Ceylon's brave effort to overcome communal trouble, the threat of insidious Communist influences, and deep-seated economic difficulties. The shrinking of distances has brought Ceylon's superb natural attractions within convenient reach of tourists, traders, and even makers of films who need lush tropical backgrounds and bright blue skies.

Here, then, is a kind of Ceylon sampler. It includes the highlights of Ceylon's history, concentrating on a few major figures; it suggests without detailed analysis the historical, economic, and sociological causes of current conditions; it briefly refers to the great cultural traditions and the promise of the future; it describes, though too briefly, the physical beauty and charm of the country.

I am grateful to the Asia Society for giving me the opportunity to write about Ceylon, where my family and I lived happily for five years. To three distinguished Ceylonese, who patiently read this book in manuscript and made many helpful comments, I extend warm thanks: the Honorable Herbert Hulugalle, Ambassador until July 1959 from Ceylon to Italy; Senator Haji A. M. A. Azeez, Member of Ceylon's Upper House and Principal of Zahira College, in Colombo; and Annesley de Silva, Counselor of Embassy, in Ceylon's Mission to Washington. They helped me to correct some of my errors and faulty interpretations, but they are, of course, not to be blamed for the errors that remain and my occasional failure to heed their advice. I also want to thank Mr. and Mrs. John Exter and Mrs. Julie d'Estournelles, my neighbors when I lived in Ceylon, who read the manuscript and gave me the benefit of their intimate knowledge of the country.

At all stages in the preparation of this book I was also helped by the reliable memory and love of Ceylon of my wife, Nancy Palmer Tresidder, who typed the final manuscript and made the line drawings which illustrate the text.

ARGUS JOHN TRESIDDER

Falls Church, Virginia
December, 1959

Contents

	Preface	v
	Map of Ceylon	x
1.	An Introduction to Sri Lanka	1
2.	The Land and Its People	16
3.	History in Legend and Fact	62
4.	Government and Politics	119
5.	The National Economy	136
6.	The Religions of Ceylon	170
7.	The Arts of Ceylon: Past and Present	188
8.	Some Sober Final Thoughts	216
	Bibliography	221
	Glossary	229
	Index	233

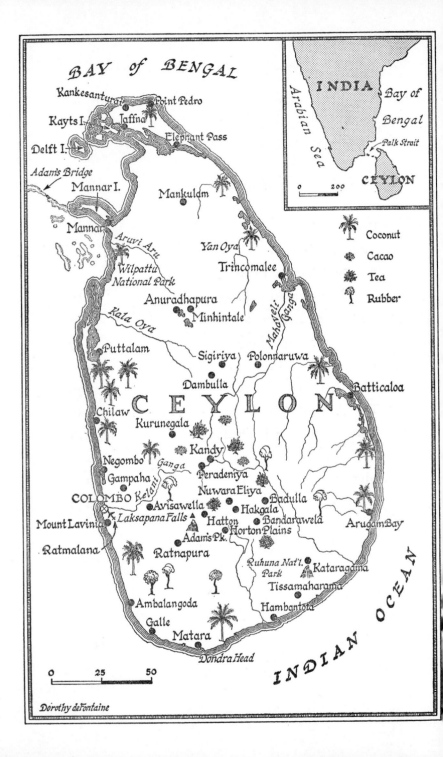

1. An Introduction to Sri Lanka

On the map of Asia, southeast of India, between approximately six and ten degrees north of the equator, is the island of Ceylon which the romantically minded say is shaped like a pearl. The Dutch, a realistic people who did a thriving business there for some hundred and fifty years, likened its shape to that of a Westphalian ham. The shank of the ham (or the stem of the pear or mango, if you will) is the Jaffna peninsula which stretches up towards India into the Bay of Bengal. Palk Strait, a narrow, shallow strip of water, separates Ceylon from India, of which it may once have been a part. The Coromandel coast of India is less than twenty-five miles from northern Ceylon. On the east, west, and south the sandy beaches of Ceylon, from which palm trees lean out over the normally gentle surf, are washed by the Indian Ocean. South of its southernmost tip there is no land except the icy shore of Antarctica. Twenty-three hundred fifty miles west of Colombo, with no land between except the tiny Maldive Islands, is Mogadiscio, Somalia, in East Africa. Eighteen hundred twenty-five miles eastward lies Singapore; only the tip of Sumatra, nearly twelve hundred miles from Colombo, comes between. It is a long way from Ceylon to any other place in the world, except India.

Ceylon is a small country, about the size of Ireland or the state of West Virginia. It is 270 miles at its greatest length from north to south and 140 miles at its greatest breadth, having an area of 25,232 square miles. Its population, rapidly increasing, was estimated at nine and a quarter million in 1959.

Famous for two thousand years as the source of spices and precious stones, Ceylon was once the favorite landfall of sailors from all parts of the world. The Greeks, the Romans, the Arabs, the Chinese, the Portuguese, the Dutch knew it well. Sindbad the Sailor landed there on two of his legendary voyages. The Roman naturalist, Pliny, made a remarkably accurate map of it in the first century A.D., though he exaggerated its size. In the thirteenth century Marco Polo gave it a circumference of twenty-four hundred miles, no doubt in tribute to its commercial importance.

Milton mentioned it in *Paradise Lost,* using the Greek name for Ceylon, Taprobane. His idea of geography was somewhat hazy, however, and he may only have been looking for the poetic name of a far-away country.

The names by which Ceylon has been known down through the centuries are an index to its status as a center of world trade and a great tourist attraction. Its first recorded name in European writing was Taprobane, reported by Alexander the Great's officers, who never got farther than the Persian Gulf, but who had heard much about the wonderful spice island to the south. Taprobane, according to the British scholar, Sir Emerson Tennent, whose two-volume study of Ceylon, published in 1859, is still the best book about the country, comes from the Sanskrit meaning "great pond" or "pond covered with red lotus." This idea, borrowed from a German writer named Lassen, Tennent rather unconvincingly says is "probably associated with the gigantic [irrigation] tanks for which Ceylon is so remarkable." Harry Williams, in *Ceylon, Pearl of the East,* says that the Greek name came from the Pali, a Vedic Aryan dialect which became the sacred language of Buddhism, "tamba vanna," meaning "copper-colored," referring to the reddish earth on which the first Aryan explorers under Vijaya landed in 543 B.C. (or, possibly, 483 B.C.). Their first capital, after which the island was named, was Tambapanni. The second

3

century Egyptian geographer, Ptolemy, called it Si-
mundu, "head of the sacred law" of Buddhism. Another name for the island, used by Ptolemy, was Salike,
which may have been a corruption of the name Sinhala,
"dwelling place of lions," preferred by the Sinhalese
descendants of the north Indian settlers. The lion of
Sinhala is the emblem of Vijaya's family because his
grandmother reputedly mated with one in Bengal and
produced Vijaya's father. In stylized form the Sinhalese
lion may be seen today on Ceylon's national flag, standing with upraised forefoot holding a sword. Sir Richard
Burton thought that the source word was not from the
Sanskrit, but from Pali, Sihalam, which meant "Place
of Jewels." Sinhala or Sihalam, with the suffix -diva,
meaning "island," through Senendiva and Silandiva,
became Serendib in Arab nomenclature and was con-
tracted to Cilao by the Portuguese, Zeilan or Ceilan
by the Dutch, and Ceylon by the English.

There were many other names: the Moors called it
Tenerisim, the "Isle of Delight," the Tamils Ilanare
and Hibernard, "Isle of Jewels," the Chinese Pa-ou-
tchow, "Island of Gems." The early Sanskrit name,
still in use today, was Lanka, "the resplendent." Lanka
is the name for Ceylon in the great Indian epic, *The
Ramayana*. The Arab name of Serendib has given a
word to the English language, "serendipity," coined by
the eighteenth century English writer, Horace Walpole, from the title of an old fairy tale, "Three Princes

4

of Serendib," in which the heroes have the faculty of making happy and unexpected discoveries by accident. "Serendipity" now means this pleasant ability to come upon good things by chance.

From the earliest times Ceylon has been the symbol of beauty and exotic romance. European writers, from Ovid to Milton, spoke of it as one of the enchanting far places of the world. Tennent believed that the city of Galle, on Ceylon's southwestern coast, may have been the site of Biblical Tarshish, from which the ships of Solomon came once in every three years, "bringing gold and silver, ivory, apes, and peacocks" (I Kings, 10, 22). Certainly the ivory, apes, and peacocks were more likely to be found in Ceylon than in Spain, where modern geographers locate Tarshish. Some early Biblical scholars believed that Noah's ark came to rest on Serendib. We know that according to Muslim legend Adam and Eve, after being expelled from Eden, lived out their lives in Ceylon, next to the Garden of Eden the most beautiful place on earth. Most travelers to Ceylon would accept this appraisal of the country's charm.

The very air of fabled Ceylon is said to have been perfumed with spices, especially cinnamon, which could be smelled miles out to sea, so that mariners knew they were coming close to the "land of the hyacinth and the ruby." Since cinnamon has no odor until after its bark has been removed and dried, however, that myth is no doubt a poetic extravagance. The busy harbor of Colombo today smells more of diesel fuel and tar than it does of spices, though the fragrance of temple flowers and the pungence of tea are fair substitutes for Milton's Sabaean odors once the visitor to Ceylon goes ashore.

Sir Emerson Tennent, in his scholarly account of early references to Ceylon, says that the island was probably not known in Europe by name until after Alexander's soldiers returned from his Indian expedition in the fourth century B.C. From that time on, the references to Ceylon, based largely at first on hearsay and full of fanciful stories and inaccurate geography, were numerous. A Seleucid ambassador named Megasthenes from ancient Syria to India told about the elephants and gold and gems of Taprobane twenty years after the death of Alexander. Adventurous Phoenician and Roman sailors added to the store of knowledge on which Pliny was able to draw, as well as the accounts of the Sinhalese ambassadors to Rome during the reign of Claudius (41–54 A.D.), who were interviewed by Pliny. Between the death of Pliny and the writing of Ptolemy's great *System of Geography* only about sixty years elapsed, but a great deal more had been learned about "the pearl on the brow of India." Ptolemy's description of Taprobane, though he made the island as large as Sumatra, proves that by the middle of the second century A.D. it had been circumnavigated by observant sailors, whose notes on the characteristics of the coastline were very detailed. In his native Alexandria, Ptolemy no doubt had many opportunities to talk to returning voyagers, from whose descriptions of Ceylon he was able to draw his famous map (based on Pliny's), used by navigators for at least a thousand years.

Not until the sixth century was a direct first-hand account of Ceylon published. Then Cosmas, a Greek merchant in Egypt, recorded the reports of Sopater, a Greek trader who had visited Ceylon and been courteously received by the Sinhalese king. Sopater wrote, "It is a great island of the ocean lying in the Indian Sea, called Sielendib by the Indians, but Taprobane by the Greeks. . . . The great island itself, according to the accounts of its inhabitants, is 900 miles long, and as many wide." He went on to tell about the busy port of Galle, whose harbor, too shallow for modern freighters, was for centuries one of the most important in the East. To it in Sopater's time came "ships from all parts of India, Persia, and Ethopia, and, in like manner, many are despatched from it." Even then there was a community of Christians, probably Nestorian Catholics, in Ceylon. Sopater was much impressed by one gem found in abundance, which he called the hyacinth—probably the sapphire—and by the coconut palms. Among the many exports of gems, spices, woods, aromatic drugs, pearls, and shells he

7

mentions elephants, which were bigger and more clever than Indian elephants and so more suitable for purposes of war.

During the following thousand years, up to the invasion of Ceylon in 1505 by the Portuguese, many accounts of Ceylon were written by Arabian, Persian, Chinese, Moorish, and European travelers, most of them adding details out of their own imaginations or from sailors' stories. The Arabs, on the whole, were more reliable reporters than the Greeks or Romans, who were inclined to embellish their tales. The Indian authors were the most inaccurate of all. Up to the nineteenth century it was commonly believed on the continent of India that Ceylon was inhabited by demons. So little was the interior of the island known even to its near neighbors that almost any stories about strange creatures, great treasures, extraordinary adventure were credible. Typical of these are the tales of Sindbad in *The Thousand and One Nights,* based on the narratives of earlier Arab voyagers, quite accurate about the coast and its people, but utterly fantastic about what happened in the mysterious interior.

One of the most interesting of the early travelers to Ceylon was Ibn Batuta, a Moor from Tangier, who arrived in Ceylon in 1347. By that time the Arabs had introduced cinnamon, regarded everywhere as a luxury almost as precious as gold, into Ceylon. There is no mention of cinnamon in any account of Ceylon before

Ibn Batuta, though even in his time Ceylon's cinnamon seems to have been considered of superior quality. Ibn Batuta, a devout Muslim, made the pilgrimage to Adam's Peak, observing "monkeys with beards like a man," the "fierce leech," still to be feared on the trail to the Peak, rhododendrons, the famous iron chains which helped pilgrims in their climb, traditionally placed there by Alexander the Great himself, and the sacred footprint which the Muslims believed was pressed into the solid rock by Adam.

The extent of early traffic between Ceylon and China is surprising. Pliny says that the Sinhalese ambassadors to Rome in the reign of Claudius claimed that their ancestors had reached China across India and the Himalayas years before the long journey was attempted by sea. The vigor and enterprise of those early Sinhalese, who certainly did not wait to be discovered, but went forth in all audacity both as merchants and as Buddhist missionaries, are remarkable indeed in the light of Ceylonese insularity today.

Like the Greek geographers, Tennent says, the Chinese thought Ceylon was much bigger than it actually is and that it was wider from east to west than from north to south. Like all travelers, they were struck by the height and singularity of Adam's Peak, long a landmark for ships approaching Ceylon. They too made the pilgrimage to the Footprint on the Peak, which they believed had been made by the first created man, whom they called Pawn-koo. The jewels of Ceylon they thought were the crystalized tears of Pawnkoo. They admired the island for its fertility and loveliness, comparing its climate with that of Siam.

The Chinese were inclined to agree with the Indians about the demons and dragons supposed to haunt the interior of the island. One Chinese writer quoted by Tennent told how foreign merchants, attracted to Ceylon by the prospect of prosperous trade, had to deal with the demons in an odd way. The diffident demons never allowed themselves to be seen, but put the things they wanted to sell in a certain place, marked with the prices they expected. The traders left money for whatever they accepted, happy not to have to look on the fearsome creatures with whom they thought they were dealing. Curiously enough, the custom of trading without contact was known in Ceylon up to the beginning of the twentieth century among the aboriginal inhabitants of the eastern coast, known as Veddahs. Out of such stories come myths. No doubt the dragons which kept early visitors to Ceylon from going inland were the *kabragoyas,* the big monitor lizards, or the crocodiles, which might easily seem to a frightened man to be full-size dragons.

When Buddhism spread to China, Ceylon's fame increased as the country peculiarly favored by Buddha, who had, according to legend, visited there three times. Especially in demand were statues of Buddha made by

Sinhalese artisans. To Ceylon Chinese emperors sent missions to learn about the organization of monasteries and to get transcripts of sacred writings. The envoys returned to China impressed by the number and excellence of the Sinhalese shrines to Buddha and the great devotion of the people to religion.

As European merchants and adventurers, especially the Venetians and Genoese, extended their explorations, they too wrote about the fabulous wealth of Serendib, the name by which Ceylon was best known after the Arab influence in the East became dominant. Marco Polo, who stopped in Ceylon on his voyage home from China in 1291, found the Moorish traders in full command of Ceylon's commercial interests. He was especially impressed by Ceylon's gems, including a ruby "one palme long and as big as a man's arme, without spot," for which Kublai Khan offered the value of a city, but was refused by the king.

These early travelers' stories about Ceylon demonstrate how important the island was in the past, not only as the source of precious commodities and the center of a flourishing civilization, but as the home, when Buddhism declined in its native country of India, of a rich and productive religious culture.

Ceylon is today still as beautiful and as well endowed with natural resources as it was when Sopater and Ibn Batuta visited it hundreds of years ago. Times have changed, of course, and cinnamon is no longer considered a gift for kings. Ceylon elephants have no military value in the era of intercontinental ballistic missiles, and the gems of Lanka have much less significance in world markets than her tea and rubber, which were unknown in Ceylon before the nineteenth century. The demons have shrunk to a handful of cave-dwelling Veddahs, and the mighty cities of the early Sinhalese, with their brazen palaces and gold-spired shrines, have fallen in ruins. Nevertheless, the glamor and mystery and romance of Ceylon are still there, untouched by such contemporary mundane things as hydroelectric power sites, Colombo Plan, UNESCO, and ICA projects, and the weary search for political stability.

Before we leave this section of impressions and conjectures to take a look at the economic and social life of the people and the provable facts of history, here are four quotations from writers in different centuries who have tried to condense into short space their impressions of Ceylon:

From *The Arabian Nights,* early tenth century, "The Sixth Voyage of Sindbad":

Now the Island Sarandib lieth under the equinoctial line, its night and day both numbering twelve hours. It measureth eighty leagues long [approximately 300 miles, though the term may have been used poetically to mean almost any distance] by a breadth of thirty and its width is bounded by a lofty mountain and a deep valley. The mountain [Adam's Peak] is conspicuous from a distance of three days and it containeth many kinds of rubies and other minerals and spice trees of all sorts. The surface is covered with emery wherewith gems are cut and fashioned; diamonds are in its rivers and pearls are in its valleys. I ascended that mountain and solaced myself with a view of its marvels which are indescribable. . .

Sindbad sailed home with a present to Haroun-al-Rashid from the King of Ceylon, "before whom are a thousand elephants, and on the battlements of whose palace are a thousand jewels. . . . The present was a cup of ruby a span high, the inside of which was embellished with precious pearls; and a bed covered with the skin of the serpent that swallowed the elephants, which skin hath spots, each like a piece of gold, and whosoever sitteth upon it never becometh diseased: and a hundred thousand *mithkals* of Indian aloe's wood; and a slave-girl like the shining full moon."

From Purchas's *Pilgrimage,* 17th Century, English:

The heavens with their dewes, the ayre with a pleasant holesomeness and fragrant freshnesse, the waters in their many rivers and fountaines, the earth diversified in aspiring hills, lowly vales, equall and indifferent plaines, filled in her inward chambers with mettalls and jewells, in her outward court and upper face stored with whole woods of the best cinnamon that the sunne seeth; besides fruits, oranges, leimons, etc. surmounting those of Spaine; fowles and beasts, both tame and wilde (among which is their elephant honoured by a natural acknowledgement of excellence of all other elephants in the world). These all have conspired and joined in common league to present unto Zeilan the chiefe of worldly treasures and pleasures, with a long

13

and healthfull life in the inhabitants to enjoye them. No marvell, then, if sense and sensualitie have heere stumbled on a paradise.

Rev. Benjamin Bailey, friend of John Keats, third Archdeacon of Colombo, 19th century:

In Eastern climes these wilder beauties glow—
The "utmost Indian Isle of Taprobane."
He who would feast his spirit blamelessly,
The world of sense and worldly joys forego,
And feel the sabbath of the soul, may know,
Amid the might of mountain scenery,
And all the glories which the eye may see,
How to be blest, or soothe his bosom's woe,
Here Nature's hand so curiously hath wrought
Her web of wonder, beautiful and bright,
That even the spirits of another world
Were with the sense of admiration caught,
Which now my grosser spirit doth delight,
And from me hath my darker feeling hurl'd.

And, finally, here is what a son of Ceylon, J. Vijaya-tunga, wrote about his beloved country on its first Independence Day, 4 February 1948:

There's a land I know where the winds do softly blow,
    And skies are kind and the fields are green;
There's a land I know where the rivers swiftly flow,
    And the heart is ravished by what is seen.

Replete with song and story is this land;
    Battle-scarred and legend-studded she:
Once peer of ancient Greece and Samarkand,
    Cathay and Ind and all lands free.

14

I love her hills; I love her winding streams;
   I love her glades and grass and fern:
My kin are there; and from afar my dreams
   Are of her glory once again.

That land is Lanka, fairest isle of all,
   Whose hills the clouds do hug and kiss:
That land is Lanka, at whose sacred call
   Our hearts do stir with pride and bliss.

There's a land I know where the winds do softly blow . . .

2.   *The Land and Its People*

A visitor to Ceylon approaching by air from Madras
might stop down at Kankesanturai, in Jaffna, and so
get his first impression of the northern part of the
island, which is quite different from other areas. He
would see the vertical trunks and broad, fan-like leaves
of the palmyra palms; the well-sweeps powered by
agile men walking up and down the beams to irrigate
the thirsty fields of tobacco, vegetables, and occasional
paddy; corrals of huge sea turtles; flocks of sheep
whose wool is so sparse that they look like goats; the
dust raised by a steady, dry wind.

As the plane resumes its flight to Colombo, it leaves
behind the old Dutch fort and crosses the shallow

lagoon of Jaffna City, in which fishermen tend their weirs. Soon it is above dense green forest, interrupted at intervals by clearings in which the emerald green of paddy stands out brightly. Where the shore curves into a bay, the plane flies over the water, in which outrigger canoes or bigger fishing boats go about their business. The plane's shadow in the clear sunshine falls on more shades of green as the shallow water near the shore shelves off to the darker green of deep water. On the sandy beaches curls a succession of white, easy breakers. Near the thatched-roof villages often appear tiny, spired white domes which the stewardess says are Buddhist shrines. The larger settlements have some red-tiled houses. All along the coast is a belt of coconut palms, whose luxuriant, spreading tops and gracefully bending trunks contrast with the solid green of the forest. The overall pattern is that of tropical fertility, marked by constantly varied greenness.

As the plane reaches Colombo, the busy, well-ordered harbor within its breakwater appears first, then the government buildings, the race-course, the red-tiled roofs of large and small residences, more coconut groves and paddy fields, the magnificent beach of Mount Lavinia, and finally the runway of Ratmalana Airport, near which working elephants may be seen padding down the road, urged on by mahouts.

The following essential statistics about Ceylon, in capsule form, may be helpful to the traveler coming in for a landing, as well as for those who make their journeys from armchairs.

LOCATION

Between 5°55′ and 9°50′ north latitude and between 79°42′ and 81°52′ east longitude.

AREA

25,332 square miles.

Greatest length: 270 miles from Point Pedro in the north to Dondra Head in the south.

Greatest breadth: 140 miles from Colombo in the west to Sagamankande in the east.

PRINCIPAL MOUNTAIN PEAKS

Pidurutalagala (Mount Pedro), 8,291 feet above sea level.

Kirigalpotta, 7,856 feet above sea level.

Totapola, 7,741 feet above sea level.

Adam's Peak, 7,360 feet above sea level.

PRINCIPAL RIVERS

Mahaveli-ganga, 206 miles.

Aruvi-aru, 104 miles.

Kala-oya, 97 miles.

Yan-oya, 94 miles.

Kelani-ganga, 87 miles.

MEAN TEMPERATURE

80° to 82° F. in the low country.

60° F. at Nuwara Eliya, 6,200 feet above sea level.

RELATIVE HUMIDITY

70 percent during the day to about 90 percent at night, about 5 percent less in the Dry Zone.

From 40 inches in the driest zones in the northwest and southeast to over 200 inches at certain places on the southwestern slopes of the hills.

Distances from Colombo to various cities of the world:

To London	6,725 miles by sea,	5,532 by air.
To New York	9,941 miles by sea,	8,974 by air.
To San Francisco	10,289 miles by sea,	10,230 by air.
To Bombay	1,042 miles by sea,	970 by air.
To Rangoon	1,249 miles by sea,	2,548 by air.
To Yokahama	5,151 miles by sea,	4,338 by air.
To Melbourne	5,380 miles by sea,	5,709 by air.
To Cape Town	5,070 miles by sea,	4,400 by air.

Topography

The palm-lined coast is broken here and there by coral reefs, sandbanks, and shoals. In the north and northwest, flanking the Jaffna peninsula, itself all but severed from the mainland, are a number of islands, of which the largest have the Dutch names of Kayts and Delft (where wild horses roam, the descendants of those brought by the Portuguese). On the northwest coast, Mannar Island stretches out like a peninsula to within eighteen miles of the farthest outpost of India. The southeastern coast is so rugged that fewer palms grow down to the sea than in other areas. On the eastern coast at the mouth of the Mahaveli-ganga is the superb natural harbor of Trincomalee, which can easily accommodate a major naval force.

From the central hills flow sixteen rivers over sixty miles in length, through dense tropical forests and rich plantations to the sea. In the south-central section is a mountainous area of more than four thousand square miles, rising from an outer belt, from two to three thousand feet above sea-level, up to the true highlands, with elevations from three to eight thousand feet. A relatively narrow coastal plain, broadening out north of the mountains, occupies the rest of the island, continuing for some distance out to sea as the Continental Shelf. A coral reef lies close to the coast, mostly submerged, breaking the force of the surf on the many beaches. In the mountains, there are jagged peaks, fertile valleys, spectacular waterfalls, and great plains, notably Horton Plains, which levels out at an elevation of seven thousand feet, and the Nuwara Eliya Plains, at six thousand feet. The high mountains come to an abrupt halt at the southern end of Horton Plains at a weirdly grand place called World's End. From the sheer precipice, dropping away some five thousand feet, the rare visitor to this strange and lonely place may look across the jungles and tea plantations all the way to the sea, sixty-five miles away.

The island of Ceylon is composed of some of the oldest rocks in the world, whose decomposition has resulted in the production of the fertile reddish soil known as laterite. In the mysterious factories of Nature, the rocks are the source of Ceylon's mineral wealth, producing quartz, feldspar, and mica. The sapphires, rubies, aquamarines, and other gem-stones, for which the island has long been renowned, wash down out of secret places into gravel banks and stream beds in the region of Ratnapura, City of Gems. Another product of Ceylon's rock formations is graphite or plumbago. In the rivers too are found small quantities of gold and, in the south-central part of the island, excellent iron-ore deposits.

The Climate

The tropical climate of Ceylon is mercifully tempered by the sea-breezes, which keep its temperatures down from the blazing heat of India's and Pakistan's long summers. Rarely does the thermometer register 90° F. in Ceylon. The high humidity, however, makes the coastal plains uncomfortably warm for those used to a gentler climate. The two monsoons—prevailing winds, from May to September from the southwest, and from late October or early November to the end of February from the northeast—modify the heat and bring cooling rains. There are no real seasons in a country whose days are nearly the same length throughout the year, whose trees are non-deciduous, and whose times of planting and harvest are scattered irregularly through the year.

The two monsoons mark the only changes in what those used to the dramatic variety of spring and fall consider a monotonous climate. March and April are the hottest months as the northeast monsoon weakens and little rain falls. The beginning of the southwest monsoon is usually marked by torrential rainstorms. The northeast monsoon has considerably less rain. In the inter-monsoon periods winds are light, and rain falls only as soft afternoon showers. From June to August rainfall in the up-country areas is heavy, and fogs lie low on the mountains. The most pleasant months in Ceylon are from August to October and from December to February, though almost never, except in the highlands during the rainy season, is there an all-day gloom. The sun shines most of nearly every day, interrupted by the rains, which usually clear away quickly. In Colombo during most of the year one can expect a daytime temperature of 86° and brilliant sunshine. At night, however, the temperature seldom goes below 70°. Cloud effects, especially near the beginnings of the monsoon periods, are stunning, and sunsets are often of great beauty.

Vegetation

As one flies over Ceylon, especially after passing above the brown plains of southern India between Madras and Trichinopoly, one's impression is of vivid greenness. Everywhere is lush vegetation, bearing witness to abundance of rain and rich soil. Over three thousand species of flowering plants and ferns, not counting the mosses and fungi, grow in the island. Some nine hundred of these plants are found only in Ceylon; the remainder may also be found in India, Madagascar, Sumatra, Java, and Mauritius, which may all have been part of a large land mass in the remote past.

Everywhere is fecund beauty: in the well-watered countryside the tender green of paddy fields, yielding two and even three crops a year; in the towns, flamboyant trees, glowing with yellow and red blossoms, the lovely frangipani trees, bougainvillea hedges, orderly beds of cannas, familiar flowers introduced by British gardeners, exotics like crotons, hibiscus (locally called "shoe-flower" because its leaves are good for polishing shoes), orchids, lantana, and the graceful palms. In the villages wherever one drives in Ceylon, houses are built among trees: plantains, arecanut, mangoes, breadfruit, jak, kitul palms, limes, and of course the ever-present coconuts. In the low country are coconut and rubber plantations; up-country are the tea estates, spreading their glossy-leaved bushes over miles of mountainside. In the jungles, as all forested areas are called, are ebony, ironwood, and satinwood trees. Ceylon jungles are never like the steamy, sinister rain-jungles of Brazil and Burma; they are usually thickly wooded forests which open out to park-like meadow-

23

lands and ponds. In the cleared parts of the highlands, where industrious men have not planted tea or paddy (on skilfully built terraces), there are many gardens very like those of England, growing cabbage, beans, beets, and other vegetables that need coolness and sun, and many flowers, including gladioli, belladonna lilies, and rich banks of poinsettias. On the high slopes rhododendron is everywhere. The rolling, treeless grasslands called *patanas* of the up-country plains are very like English downs or, some say, the Scottish highlands. In the dry zones, the lush vegetation thins, and there is less color. In Jaffna, even the coconut palms change to the hardy palmyras, and the exuberant greens become the dusty browns of southern India.

The variety and beauty of Ceylon's trees, shrubs, ferns, and flowers may be observed in two excellent botanical gardens, one the world-famous Peradeniya Gardens, near Kandy, the other at Hakgalle, near Nuwara Eliya. A third, sea-level garden, at Gampaha, not far from Colombo, was the source of Ceylon's first rubber-trees.

The Fauna

Amidst this luxuriant plant life thrive many animals, birds, reptiles, and insects, which multiply with the same astonishing fertility that marks all living things, including man, in Ceylon. Only the elephants, whose intelligence and quick adaptation to captivity have been known for many centuries, are in danger of dying out. In 1956 it was estimated that fewer than a thousand wild elephants still survive in the dwindling jungles of Ceylon. The Ceylon elephant has small ears, usually no tusks, and five toes on each forefoot, four on each hind foot. In the past, the rare tusker with five toes on each foot was treated as a royal beast, like the great King Dutthagamini's beloved Kandula. Only a few are left today, notably the huge tusker belonging to the Temple of the Tooth in Kandy, which has the honor of carrying the Tooth Relic during certain ceremonies. The elephants, long sought by hunters and slaughtered by the thousands, are now protected by strict game laws, and the last elephant *kraal* or round-up was held in 1951. Since elephants seldom breed in captivity, the problem of replacing the patient, powerful creatures which still do much of the heavy work, such as moving logs and clearing jungle, is already becoming acute. One of the most exciting experiences visitors to Ceylon have is to come upon working elephants clanking their chains along the roads or to watch one of the many *peraheras* or ceremonial parades, loved by all Ceylonese, which would be incomplete without caparisoned elephants.

Among the wild creatures which are in little danger of extinction are *sambhur* elks, wild buffalo, wild boar, bears, leopards, jackals, crocodiles, monkeys, and several species of deer, particularly the beautiful spotted

25

deer, whose stags may have three-foot antlers. There are no lions in Ceylon, except on the national flag and in the excellent Colombo Zoo, and no tigers, though they are quite common in India, only a few miles away. Travelers get quite used to seeing mongooses cross in front of their cars, as well as the giant lizard called the *kabragoya,* which may be more than six feet long, and the iguana, which the Sinhalese call the *talagoya.* Monkeys are found nearly everywhere except near settled areas. The smallest species is the brown macaque or *rilawa.* The four other varieties are all *wanderoos,* big grey animals with beetling black eyebrows, white beards, short head-hair that looks as if it had been given a crew cut. They swing from tree to tree along the roads; their presence emphasizes the loneliness of the ruined cities. One of the most fascinating of Ceylon's many creatures is the loris, a dainty, big-eyed lemur about the size of a squirrel whose fantastically slow movements give it the name of the Ceylon sloth. Makers of love potions use tears from the enormous eyes of the loris, made to weep by being held close to a flame.

Pythons are found in the jungles. Cobras, which are held in reverence by both Buddhists and Hindus, and the vicious *tic polongas* or Russell's vipers are the only poisonous land snakes. They may be found anywhere, including the gardens of luxurious bungalows in the cities. The big rat snake, which looks like the cobra without a hood, is, like the American black snake, helpful to farmers and quite harmless. The only snakes that visitors are likely to see, however, are the cobras in the baskets of Muslim snake-charmers.

Ceylon has over four hundred species of birds, some forty of which are found nowhere else in the world. Tourists who arrive in Ceylon by sea are impressed by the fact that in Colombo's harbor the birds which greet their ships are crows rather than gulls. These strident, bold, clever birds, which have a look of criminal cunning that no other crows seem to have, are the plague of urban Ceylon. Visitors who do not get far from the towns may feel that bird-life is meager, except for the villainous crows. If they watch, however, they will catch sight of the gorgeous blue stork-billed kingfisher or the plain little pied robin, with bluish grey rather than red breast, or the mynah, with glossy black head and yellow diamonds near his eyes, or even an occasional green bee-eater and the big, fan-tailed, rusty-colored crow-pheasant. In the dry-zone jungle preserves, one near Anuradhapura, called Wilpattu National Park, the other in the southeastern corner, the Ruhuna National Park, may be seen a tremendous variety of birds: for example, pea-fowl, whose harsh meowing is a common sound, hornbills, red-wattled lapwings, which warn of intruders by shrill cries of "Did-he-do-it?", Brahminy kites, paradise fly-catchers with long tail feathers, jungle-fowl, the

27

colorful progenitors of our domestic chickens, and the splendid green imperial pigeons.

In the rivers and in the sea are many kinds of fish. Most common is the sea-fish called *seer,* which tastes like salmon, served so often in Ceylon hotels and rest-houses that travelers may grow weary of it. Much more satisfying are the excellent crabs, prawns, and lobsters found along the coasts. In the Bay of Bengal are caught big sea-turtles, whose meat is much loved by some Tamils. The tortoiseshell which is made into combs and boxes is taken from the hawksbill, another sea-turtle. Deep sea fishing off Ceylon is seldom exciting. Fishermen in frail outrigger canoes bring in big, but passive fish caught on hand-lines or in nets. Sharks sometimes appear off the coast, though usually not within the barrier reef. Opinions differ about whether or not they are man-eaters. Swimmers seem not to be afraid of them, even the increasing tribe of skin-divers, who have found the marine life off the reefs of Ceylon among the most interesting in the world. A book, written in 1957, *The Reefs of Taprobane, Underwater Adventures Around Ceylon,* by Arthur C. Clarke, bears eloquent witness to the beauty and fascination of Ceylonese waters. Among the extraordinary fishes of Ceylon are the climbing fish, which can cross open country and even climb trees, the flower parrot, a brilliant fish found near the reefs, and the singing fish of Batticaloa, on the eastern coast, which on moonlight nights produce an eerie hum.

The People

The last census of Ceylon was made in March, 1953. At that time the total population was 8,097,895, of whom 4,268,730 were males and 3,829,165 females. By March 1956, the estimated population was 8,735,-000. By 1959, the number had grown to an estimated 9,250,000. More than three-fifths of these live in the Wet Zone, the southwest quarter of the island. In the Dry Zone north of the mountains, which once was the center of the great Sinhalese civilization, the residents, thinned out by malaria and migration to healthier sections of the island, are once more increasing in number, thanks to malaria control and resettlement projects.

The government's vigorous program of public health which was accelerated after World War II, dramatically cut the death-rate. The birth-rate, already high, combined with the decreased death-rate to give Ceylon a rate of natural increase of nearly 3 percent a year, among the highest in the world today. This explosive population growth of almost three million between 1946 and 1959 has already caused economic pressure. The richly productive island is beginning to have difficulty in supporting its burgeoning population. The density of population in 1953 of 324 persons per square mile is already more than that of New York

State (316) and that of India (305). Poverty and famine, less known in Sri Lanka than in other parts of crowded Asia, are an increasing threat today.

Racial Organization

The complexity of Ceylon's racial organization (perhaps ethnic is a better word than racial) is evident from the following table, based on the census of 1953:

Low-country Sinhalese	3,469,512
Kandyan Sinhalese	2,147,193
Ceylon Tamils	884,703
Indian Tamils	974,098
Ceylon Moors	463,963
Indian Moors	47,462
Burghers and Eurasians	45,950
Malays	25,464
Veddahs	803
Europeans	6,508
Others	32,239

The Sinhalese

More than two-thirds of the population is Sinhalese, claiming descent from the original north-Indian settlers, though as we have seen the Sinhalese from Vijaya onward intermarried extensively with Tamils. They speak Sinhalese, an Indo-European language derived from the Sanskrit. About 93 percent of the Sinhalese are Hinayana Buddhists; the rest are Christians. The Kandyan Sinhalese are those tracing their ancestry to the highland families who resisted both

Tamil and European invaders. The Kandyans are a proud, independent people, confident that their culture is purer than that of their low-country brothers, who surrendered to foreign domination. There is, however, no basis for racial differentiation. Dr. N. D. Wijese-kera, a Sinhalese anthropologist, says that "if racially there exists any notable difference between the upland and lowland folk, it may be with regard to the higher percentage of Vedda and Dravidian blood in the upland element of the Sinhalese."

The Kandyan Sinhalese have departed less than the low-country Sinhalese from ancient customs. For example, a code of civil law governs the Kandyans which is different in many respects from the code of the low-land Sinhalese, based on Roman-Dutch laws. There are fewer Christians among the Kandyans than among the low-country Sinhalese. Caste organization is still stronger up-country than in the more sophisticated urban communities along the coast. The low-country Sinhalese have been more receptive to industrial, commercial, and social changes than the Kandyans, many of whom look back with regret on the passing of their feudal privileges. The principal up-country industry, tea, has long been under the control of the British, who imported Indian Tamil laborers, better suited than the Sinhalese to hard manual work. Both Kandyan and low-country Sinhalese adhere to strong clan relationships, often arranging marriages according to family rather than to individual considerations. The caste system, much more flexible than among the Hindus, is nevertheless very important in the social structure, in spite of the tendency of many educated Sinhalese to disparage its influence. The Sinhalese people as a whole are an easy-going, friendly, sweet-natured people, fond of ceremonies and celebrations of all kinds, fun-loving and humorous, gentle (though quick to anger which results in an astonishingly high national homicide rate), and unaggressive.

The Tamils

A little less than a quarter of the total population of Ceylon is Tamil. More than half of this ethnic group are recent immigrants from south India or the descendants of immigrants after 1830; they make up most of the labor population of the estates. The Ceylon Tamils are the descendants of early settlers from India, some of whom may even have antedated the arrival of Vijaya. During the hundreds of years of attempted and periodically successful conquest of Ceylon by Cholas, Pandyans, and Cheras from south India, their influence was great not only socially and culturally but racially as well. Wijesekera points out that the practice of intermarriage between Sinhalese and Tamils grew when the two races lived together peacefully, especially in the later Kandyan kingdom. The two groups are nearly endogamous today, living in near proximity only in urban areas. Between them has developed an interracial rivalry that in 1958 burst into violence.

The Indian Tamils, most of whom have not been accepted as citizens of Ceylon, are the cause of friction between the governments of Ceylon and India. Ceylon, trying to keep its population growth down, has refused to naturalize more than fifty thousand of the more than a million Indian Tamils now resident in Ceylon, but since India will not repatriate them, their status is under dispute. The children of Indian Tamils born in Ceylon do not automatically receive Ceylonese citizenship.

Tamils speak a Dravidian language, unrelated to Sinhalese. The two languages of Ceylon, using different scripts, existed side by side without serious trouble until Independence. As long as the British were in control, English was the official language (though it was never spoken by more than about 10 percent of the population), and among the educated classes, both Sinhalese and Tamil, English became more important than the indigenous languages. After 1948, a number of very prominent Ceylonese had to brush up on their native tongues, which once more, as the spirit of nationalism grew, became popular. Like India after independence, Ceylon passed laws restoring the *swabhasha,* as the local languages are called, to first place in schools and official communication, but allowing for

33

the passage of several years to prepare for the changes. Meanwhile, English continued as the chief means of communication at government and professional level and in the University.

Both Sinhalese and Tamil were fostered, though English remained the official language until July 7, 1956, when Parliament passed a law making Sinhalese the one official language of Ceylon. This law, together with other actions of the dominant Sinhalese group, has effectively weakened the influence of the large Tamil minority. Symbolical of economic and social competition, the language issue, used by some selfish politicians and fomenters of religious and political hatreds to further special interests, as well as by honest but overzealous patriots, was at the center of the bitter communal discord that shook the island in 1958.

Most Tamils are Hindus, chiefly of the Saivite cult, though about 10 percent are Christians. They have maintained the culture of south India with very little change. The Indian Tamils usually keep in close touch with their home villages in India and consider themselves part of the ethnic pattern of the Tamil race rather than Ceylonese. Ceylon Tamils, of course, owe no loyalty to India, but do hold to the caste system and conservative traditions of their Indian kinsmen. Concentrated in the north and east of Ceylon, they have kept in closer touch with India than with the Sinhalese, separated from them not only by religion, language, and social customs, but also for many years by the almost deserted Dry Zone and jungles. The Sinhalese, long removed in time and distance from their north Indian ancestors, have developed independently.

The Ceylon Tamils, who have by constant hard work and resourceful methods of cultivation compelled the poorly watered soil of the Jaffna peninsula and the east coast to yield crops, are generally more industrious and thrifty than the Sinhalese. They have a traditionally high respect for education and have pursued book-learning with the same energy and zeal that they display in raising food. Jaffna Tamils have sought advancement and professional distinction in the face of great discouragement. As a result they are represented in far greater proportion than their numbers warrant in government, the civil service, and the professions.

The Moors

The Ceylon Moors are descendants of the Arab merchants who gradually took over the profitable spice trade after the eighth century and held it until the coming of the Portuguese. Since they brought few women with them on their trading voyages, they married local women and formed Muslim communities. Today the Ceylon Moors are most heavily concentrated

35

on the eastern coast; many of them live in Colombo, making their livings as shopkeepers and traders. They are speakers of Tamil even in Sinhalese areas, and practically without exception they are Muslims. Unaffected by the caste system that governs the social status of both the Sinhalese and Tamils, the Moors keep their group identity and hold to the Muslim customs, especially the segregation of their women, many of whom still practice purdah. Many of the men wear red fezzes like those popular in the Middle East.

Indian Moors, among them gold-turbaned members of the Borah sect from Bombay, are recent arrivals, many of them temporary immigrants, most merchants and traders who live in Colombo. Wijesekera says that the light-eyed, fair-skinned, tall, handsome members of this group are really of Turkish extraction. They are probably from north India; the true Indian Moors are from south India. Other Muslims are the Malays, who were brought in as mercenaries by the Dutch. They have intermarried so freely with the Sinhalese and Tamils that they are fast disappearing as an identifiable group. Another small but conspicuous community of Muslims is known as Afghans or Baluchis. They are big, powerful men, usually from Pakistan rather than from Afghanistan, who stride about in baggy cotton trousers, long-tailed turbans, and flowing blouses, over which are worn colored waistcoats. The Afghans are often money-lenders, who charge very high rates of interest and are physically feared by their less robust clients.

The Burghers

The Burghers are descendants of the Dutch and other European employees of the Dutch East India Company who intermarried with the Sinhalese. The descendants of Portuguese–Sinhalese marriages have tended to be absorbed by the Sinhalese, but the true Burghers have zealously kept apart from other groups, considering themselves Europeans in culture and origin. Few Burghers marry outside their own class-conscious community. They generally wear western clothing, scorning *sarees, sarongs, sherwanis,* and other non-European costumes. Originally they spoke Dutch, but are now fluent speakers of English. The British tended to favor the Western-oriented Burghers in their government of Ceylon, encouraging them to enter the civil service and the professions, in which they are well represented today, though in number they are less than half of one percent of the total population. Since Ceylon became independent, however, the Burghers have begun to lose their privileged position and are now finding life hard among the Sinhalese. Many of them, fearing the threat to their social and cultural identity, are migrating to Australia. The Burghers are urban dwellers. Most of them are Protestant Christians, though some are Catholics.

There was little intermarriage between the British and the Sinhalese and Tamils. The few Eurasians, offspring of British and Ceylonese parents, are usually counted among the Burghers, but not by the Burghers themselves, who proudly claim legitimate descent in the male line from carefully restricted ancestors.

The Veddahs

The Veddahs, now almost extinct as a pure race, are descendants of the aboriginal tribes who inhabited Ceylon before the coming of the Indian settlers. Most of them have been absorbed by the Sinhalese. The few surviving genuine Veddahs live under extremely primitive conditions in the jungles of eastern Ceylon. These forest-dwellers, who, according to Williams, "have maintained standards of truth, courtesy, marital fidelity, and simple kindness that the modern world has all but discarded," are of great anthropological interest. Very sympathetic and charming stories about the Veddahs may be found in the books of the Burgher physician, Dr. Richard Spittel.

Other Racial Groups

Other small communities in the fascinating racial composite of Ceylon are Europeans, mainly British, Parsees from Bombay, Goanese, a few Chinese, some Kaffirs, originally imported as slaves or soldiers by the Sinhalese and later employed as musicians in regimental bands by the European conquerors, and a few south Indian, Telegu-speaking gypsies known as *Kuravans*.

Racial Distinctions

The typical Sinhalese has a big, broad head. His lips are somewhat thick, his hair black and slightly wavy, his eyes dark, his nose narrow and straight. His skin color varies from brown to fair, and he usually has abundant body hair. He is short in stature. The typical Tamil is of medium height and slight build. He is usually darker in complexion than the Sinhalese, has a long head and narrow face, a rather broad nose, and sparse hair on face and body. But these are descriptions of anthropological characteristics that are in actual fact hard to distinguish in Ceylon today. There are other types: heavy-set, hairy Tamils and fine featured, thin-lipped, fair people, who, like a few with Negroid blood, may be either Sinhalese or Tamil. Intermarriage between the two chief ethnic groups, less common today than in the past, has made the physical differences between them hard to identify. Except that Tamils tend to have somewhat darker skin than the Sinhalese, casual observers find it almost impossible to distinguish between them. Their names, however, are easy means to identify the various communities: Sinhalese names end in -e and -a, as in Jayamanne, Hulugalle, Senanayake, Jayawardana. Many Sinhalese have Portuguese family names like de Silva, Perera, and Fer-

39

nando. Tamil names usually end in -m, -n, -y, -ai, or -rajah: Pararajasingham, Coomaraswamy, Vaithia- nathan, Wignerajah. Some Tamils took the names of American missionaries: Barnes, Green, Niles, Wilson. Occasionally a Tamil name is a real jaw-breaker: Thiruganasampandamuthiunainar Pillai. Moors have Middle Eastern names like Azeez, Ahamed, Saheed. The Burghers, who often physically resemble the Sin- halese, have Dutch and other European names: Van Langenberg, Vandersmagt, Jansz, Sansoni, Collette, Garvin.

All the communities are clearly differentiated through religious practices, family customs, and to a lesser ex- tent dress.

Caste Systems

The Sinhalese caste system, though of Indian origin, has not developed in the same way, mainly because of the early conversion of Ceylon to Buddhism. Thus there is no priestly caste corresponding to the Brah- mans. The organization of Sinhalese castes is purely secular, and though the system has weakened, espe- cially in urban areas, it still has many of the practices that Robert Knox observed during his captivity in Kandy in the 17th century. He described the "divers and sundry casts or degrees of quality, which is not according to their riches or places of honour the King promotes them to, but according to their descent and blood. And whatsoever this honour is, be it higher or lower, it remains hereditary from generation to generation. They abhor to eat or drink, or intermarry with any of inferior quality to themselves."

The structural origins of the castes are probably the castes, tribal groups, and guilds of India. Functionally, castes were in the past and to some slight extent are today differentiated by occupational or ceremonial responsibilities, or both. Caste no longer has much connection with occupation, and the ceremonial duties have almost disappeared except among the Kandyan aristocrats. Though little is left of the actual special privileges and responsibilities beyond the traditions, much of the old relationship between one caste and another is still preserved. Legal distinctions associated with caste have been abolished, but especially in the less sophisticated areas caste tabus often still apply to marriage, home life, and food. Bryce Ryan, who has made the only comprehensive modern study of Ceylon's caste system, says, concerning the survival of caste today, that "symbols of social distance vary widely by region, but range from deferential expressions in salutation to proscription of articles of clothing and ornament, and insistence on worshipful behavior toward the higher caste."

Caste among the Sinhalese is a little like the fraternity system on an American university campus. Nonmembers, however scornful of the system, often have a sense of deprivation, of not being admitted to the social hierarchy. Members of the various chapters differ in some degree about which fraternity is "best," but most are aware of a loose kind of rank, and one group which has more than its share of athletic and organization leaders is usually recognized as outstanding, the others taking position behind it. Interfraternity relationships (including traditional monopoly of certain campus offices), though much less serious than intercaste problems of marriage, precedence at official functions, and the like, would be quite understandable to caste-conscious Sinhalese. Like the fraternity system, too, caste is of increasingly less importance. Visitors to Ceylon are advised not to be too curious about this very delicate subject since the Ceylonese are reluctant to talk about what they are sure Western people will never understand and what is for them a matter of pride mixed with some embarrassment.

Though no non-Sinhalese will ever fully comprehend the nuances of Sinhalese caste, and though any attempt by an outsider to explain it is open to the charge of insensitive meddling, the picture of the Sinhalese would be incomplete without some mention of caste. The following account is largely based on the study by Bryce Ryan, an American sociologist who lived several years in Ceylon.

Ryan lists twenty-five contemporary Sinhalese castes (and a number of subcastes of the first three), some of them found only in the highlands, others only in the low country. There is by no means general acceptance of Ryan's arbitrary order of rank. For example, some members of the *Karava* or fisher caste believe that they are descendants of the Indian warrior caste, the *Kshatrias,* and are therefore higher in rank than any of the other Ceylonese castes. The first four Sinhalese castes, according to Ryan, are *Goyigama,* cultivators of the soil, *Karava,* fishermen, *Salagama,* cinnamon peelers, and *Durava,* toddy tappers. Below them he ranks the artisans, tailors, *dhobies* (washermen to higher castes), potters, barbers, tom-tom beaters, dancers, and so on, down to the *Rodiyas* or outcastes.

The *Rodi* caste, which compares with India's untouchables, is a depressed group which makes its living as scavengers, beggars, jugglers, and prostitutes. They are romantically believed to have once been a noble caste of king's hunters. A lazy hunter on one occasion served human flesh instead of venison to the king, who in horror degraded all *Rodiyas.* In later years kings punished their high-caste followers who displeased them by giving their wives and daughters to the *Rodiyas.* The *Rodi* women are notable for their beauty and proud carriage, supposedly inherited from their aristocratic and unwilling ancestors. One of the outcaste conditions placed upon the Rodiyas was that both men and women must go uncovered above the waist. Colombo shops sell postcards of bare-breasted *Rodiya*

43

beauties, but travelers will look in vain for a Ceylonese Bali since the clothing tabu has long since been abandoned.

The *Goyigamas* or "*G*'s," as they are often called by those who like to deprecate caste, comprise about half the Sinhalese population, the great majority of whom are peasant farmers. In general, however, the wealthiest and most powerful members of most communities are likely to be *Goyigamas*. For example, most cabinet ministers and holders of other key government positions since Independence have been *Goyigamas*. Ranking high among the *Goyigama* subcastes are the *Radalas*, the Kandyan chiefs, who still command grave respect and who have often been a significant factor in the formation of governments. *Radalas* normally marry only other *Radalas*, or members of another aristocratic subcaste, the *Mudali*, "leaders of the people."

The relatively high positions of the *Goyigamas*, the *Karavas*, the *Salagamas*, and the *Duravas* in Ceylonese society have been attained in large part through commercial initiative. The *Karavas*, for example, have been successful in business and have more easily adjusted to changing conditions than other groups. Much of the economic strength of Ceylon is in their hands. The *Salagamas*, because of their connection with the prosperous cinnamon trade, came into political and economic prominence, as did the *Duravas*, who made their living from the palms which supplied the island's popular drinks, toddy and arrack.

As Western concepts of classless society have become popular among the Ceylonese who consider themselves emancipated, caste has lost many of its external manifestations. Many lower-caste men now wear *baniyans,* or undershirts (without shirts), in defiance of the old ban on covering for the upper body. Marriages, of course, continue to be controlled by strict caste rules, but at public meetings, during worship in the temples, and in schools there is no longer segregation by caste. At an old-fashioned up-country wedding-feast, however, caste distinctions are sometimes as rigorous as in the past: only *Goyigamas* may sit at the table; if a lower-caste person sits in the presence of a *Goyigama,* he must use a low stool; a *Goyigama* cannot take food from anyone of a lower caste; when they address each other, the *Goyigama* uses pronouns indicative of his superior position and expects words of respect and honor in return.

Caste continues to be useful to politicians in much the way that American party workers make use of racial or religious groups in local politics. The Ceylonese government insists that caste has no legal status, but in actual practice caste plays a considerable part in governmental operations, both through higher-caste favoritism and discrimination against the lower castes. In the public services, education, and the courts, however, discrimination is almost non-existent, and it is evident that other caste barriers are rapidly breaking down. At the University of Ceylon students mix in deliberate disregard of caste, disapproving of any discussion on the subject. Nevertheless, as Ryan points out, some students of village origin are tormented by feelings of hereditary inferiority, and practically all graduates quietly accept family decisions concerning their marriages, which are almost inevitably within caste boundaries.

Among the Tamils the caste system, entirely different from that of the Sinhalese, continues to be powerful (though modified by various influences). The Tamils seem to be less influenced by Western ideas of equality than the urban Sinhalese, so far as restrictions imposed by caste are concerned. The Indian Tamils divide up, like south Indians, among the various subcastes of the four caste categories and the *Panchamas* or outcastes: the *Brahmans,* the priests, who are thought to spring from the head of Brahma; the *Kshatriyas,* kings and warriors, who sprang from Brahma's arms; the *Vaisyas,* merchants and farmers, from Brahma's thighs; and the *Sudras,* or laborers, without divine origin, whose duty is to serve the other castes. Within the castes strict endogamy is usual, and the relationship between higher and lower castes among the Tamils is similar in social behavior and significance to that of the Sinhalese.

46

Other Ceylonese communities have no caste organization, though the *Goyigamas* recognize the Veddahs as one of their subcastes. Catholic Sinhalese profess no caste, but certain caste-like distinctions remain among them. Christian Tamils do not abandon their castes. Burghers and Europeans are treated as "trousered gentlemen" by villagers, who consider that their light skins, trousers, and other symbols of power command the respect due the highest caste. The Moors live outside the caste system, but are well adjusted to its practice among their neighbors.

Class Distinctions

In addition to caste, class distinctions which are unrelated to caste are important among the Ceylonese. As we have seen, the growth of an English-speaking middle-class under the British eventually resulted in demands for political self-determination. The difference today is very great between those who customarily wear trousers, speak English, have modern ideas picked up in British-influenced schools or brought in by newspapers and books or, perhaps, by Marxist dialecticians—and the lower class in sarongs, without shoes, many of them still illiterate. The passion for English, which has been diminished by the nationalist demand for indigenous languages, was prompted by the universal ambition to get secure positions either in government or in commercial firms which put a premium on bilingual facility. The use of English became a mark of social achievement. The poorest families made sacrifices so that their sons could aspire to shoes and trousers and positions commanding respect and good dowries from prospective wives. Even the girls learned English if they could because it would improve their matrimonial attractiveness. The privileged position of English has already deteriorated, but for some time to come it will still be an important factor in class differentiation.

The middle class is divided into two parts: the lower middle class, clerks, newspaper reporters, assistants in trading houses, school teachers, and others with no more than a high school education, who will probably never earn more than from $75 to $100 a month; and the upper middle class, university teachers, doctors, lawyers, and government officials who have had university education and earn up to $400 a month. The lower group tends to be envious of the upper. Its members are more likely to be impressed by rabble-rousing political speakers than the masses, who are so accustomed to meagre existence and caste inferiority that they normally have little resentment against those more fortunate. The members of this lower class, servants, menial workers in the cities, estate laborers, and peasant farmers, wear sarongs, their torsos usually uncovered, and go barefoot. They speak only Tamil or Sinhalese and live mainly on rice and cheap vegetable curries. They dwell in mud-huts with *cadjan* (palm-thatched) roofs. A real upper class, unless the Kandyan aristocrats and a few "ruling families," both highland and lowland, might be so-called, does not exist. At the top level of the upper middle class are the distinguished professional people, political leaders, and senior civil servants, but no group has emerged to take the place of the British, Dutch, and Portuguese "masters." Class solidarity, such as is sought by the Communists, continues to be weak because of the persistence of caste loyalties, which cut through class divisions based on economic and educational advantages.

One of the most extraordinary phenomena of Ceylonese society, which should be a stabilizing influence, is the prestige that goes with government service. Young men who aspire to be civil servants get over their susceptibility to radical political doctrines as soon as they rise high enough in the government bureaucracy to have the sense of security which is their goal.

The Family Unit

The basic unit of Sinhalese society is the family, which is part of the larger relationship of the caste. Within the castes are broad family groups, known as *Ge*, with distinctive names, usually different from the conventional family names. The *Ge* name, which includes symbols of ancient family honors, place of

49

origin, and position within the caste, does not identify kinsmen, but establishes status. It is mainly useful in determining the suitability of prospective husbands or wives.

Marriages, the most important of all social events, are taken very seriously in Ceylon. So deeply involved in problems of caste, intracaste level, and finances are marriage contracts that only rarely do young people in love defy parental authority and marry unconventionally. Though personal preference is not ignored as frequently as in the old days, the social and financial eligibility of a potential mate is of far greater significance than previous acquaintance. Romantic marriages occur, chiefly because young people, especially in the University, have more social contact than in the past. Compatibility based on mutual interests and backgrounds has become important, particularly among Ceylonese in frequent contact with Westerners. For the most part, however, parents and relatives go about the solemn business of selecting husbands or wives, for those who will carry on family traditions, very much as they always have in Ceylon. Four conditions are all but inevitable: 1) both boy and girl must belong to the same caste (marriages between Sinhalese and Tamils, of course, are very rare); 2) the bride must be a virgin; 3) the bride must be younger than her husband; 4) their horoscopes must be harmonious. Average age for marriage in urban areas is about twenty-eight for men, twenty-two for women. In rural areas marriages usually occur at an earlier age.

Horoscopes are cast for nearly all marriages (as well as before important business transactions, journeys, and the like). If the conjunction of planets evident in the horoscopes of the prospective bride and groom is not favorable, it is assumed that they would not make a satisfactory marriage physically or temperamentally. Marriages are often arranged by brokers, who are paid for discovering suitable mates. The Sinhalese prefer marriage between cross-cousins: a man and his mother's brother's daughter or his father's sister's daughter, but he is not permitted to marry his mother's sister's daughter or his father's brother's daughter. After the proper person is found, the dowry to be paid by the bride's family is settled. A well-to-do boy with job security can command a substantial dowry. A girl whose family cannot afford a dowry may not find a husband unless she has had a good education or is very beautiful.

The Sinhalese husband is dominant in his family, assuming the authority over his wife formerly exerted by her father. Except in sophisticated city families, the wife defers in all ways to her lord, walking a few steps behind him, never sitting in his presence or in that of his friends, doing all the household work while her master takes his ease. Divorce, especially among the Kandyan Sinhalese, has always been easy, and under

Kandyan law, a marriage may still be dissolved by mutual consent. The Kandyan divorce rate is considerably higher than among low-country Sinhalese, who are more strongly influenced by Western legal codes, which make divorce difficult.

The Tamil family system is somewhat different from the Sinhalese. The unit itself is larger, consisting not only of parents and unmarried children, but of married sons and their families. The same strict caste regulations govern marriages, and brides are subordinated to their husbands' family groups, particularly to mothers-in-law. Both the Tamils and the Moors seclude their women more than the Sinhalese.

In summary, both the Sinhalese and the Tamils are family-centered and loyal to their caste groups. Both are conservative, behaving according to traditional patterns. Both are courteous and friendly, but the Sinhalese are more fun-loving, easy-going, and proud; the Tamils are more frugal, serious, energetic, and industrious. The Tamils tend to be more vigorous than the Sinhalese in their pursuit of education, and by virtue of driving ambition they earn more than their proportionate share of responsible positions in government. Both have produced great patriots and persuasive speakers; the Sinhalese are perhaps more skilled in political matters, the Tamils in business.

It should not be forgotten that these are generalized comments that apply more to the rural areas than to the cities. The differences between Sinhalese and Tamil are much less distinct in the cities, where they live together, than in the segregated villages. In the cities too Western influences have made many changes in traditional views. Travel and education abroad and the increased contact with new ideas through books, magazines, and newspapers and many visitors have already had great influence on attitudes among the city-dwellers. It will be many years, however, before the rural Ceylonese, who make up 85 percent of the population, significantly change.

Clothing and Food

Most Ceylonese men, except the "trousered" class, wear *sarongs* which are tubes of cotton cloth, of any color, but generally white, with panels of grey or some brighter color down the back, ingeniously twisted at the waist into a sort of skirt; shirts, sometimes a screaming pink or orange in color, or *baniyans,* except where caste regulations prescribe no covering; and when really dressed up, neat white jackets over white shirts and sarongs. Laborers may wear simple breech cloths. The standard national costume for the middle class, which has become increasingly popular, consists of a white *sarong* and a long white collarless shirt, buttoned to the neck, hanging to mid-thigh, and a narrow, often embroidered stole or stock around the neck, the ends untied. The prescribed official evening wear of the cocktail set, who in daytime normally wear Western-style suits, shirts, and ties, is an adaptation of the Indian *sherwani,* a mid-thigh length black or white jacket, buttoned all the way to the neck, worn over white trousers or jodhpurs. A few unsophisticated older men of high caste still wear their hair in a *conde* or bun, above which grandly sits a semicircular tortoise-shell comb.

The women wear either *sarees,* six or seven yards of cloth, 45 inches wide, draped over blouses, or *camboys,* sarong-like skirts, and tight little bodices, buttoned in front, which leave an inch or two of exposed midriff. Middle-class women always wear *sarees.* Party *sarees* are often of costly, lovely silk, bordered in gold paterns, which may be draped in many graceful ways. Tamil women of the lower class usually wear a modification of the *saree,* often without a blouse. When foot-covering of any kind is used by the poorer classes, it is a simple sandal. Well-to-do men wear Western shoes and the women fancy sandals.

The staple of all Ceylonese households is rice. It is served with curries—fish, vegetable, or meat stews highly seasoned with chillies and spices—and in various other Ceylonese specialties such as *pilau, mouille, buriani,* and *lampries. Buriani,* for example, is made from rice, lean mutton, *ghee* (buffalo milk butter), onions, cinnamon, cardamon, cloves, rampa, lemon-grass, and saffron. With it is usually served an onion *sambol,* very hot to Western palates, made of Bombay onions, red onions, green peppers or chillies, and lime juice. The *pilau,* familiar in various forms to travelers in Asia, is made of rice, sometimes colored yellow with saffron, flavored with cinnamon, cardamons, and onions, and served with raisins, cashew nuts (called *cadju* nuts in Ceylon), chopped boiled eggs, and bits of crisp bacon. A favorite Sinhalese dish is a mixture obtained by grinding chillies, salt, onions, and dried fish from the Maldive Islands.

Meat is eaten only by the more affluent and those who have no dietary scruples against beef or pork or any once-living creature (strict Hindus and Buddhists cannot even eat eggs, which may be fertile). Fish and other seafood are fairly plentiful. Jak and bread-fruit are eaten in season, as are oranges, mangoes, mangosteens, rambutans, and durians. Papayas, limes, and bananas are plentiful. Some wheat flour, imported, and local cereals like *kurakkan* are eaten. Coconut milk or shredded coconut is included with most meals. Tea is the universal drink.

Education

The desire for education in Ceylon amounts almost to an obsession. The poorest peasant can dream of a secure, respected position for his children, who through education may compete for government service at various levels. Middle-class ambition for a proper place in society, which can command a good dowry or engage the attention of a well-fixed young man's family, may be achieved by fulfillment of certain educational standards, up through the University, perhaps even through graduate or professional study abroad. The result of this emphasis on education, beyond doubt a product of the British period, is that Ceylon has the highest literacy rate in Asia outside of Japan and the Philippines. According to the UNESCO publication, "World Communications, 1956," Japan has an illiteracy rate of only 2–3 percent, the Philippines, 34–40 percent, Formosa and Ceylon 40–45 percent. The Ceylon government's own estimate of its national literacy is higher.

In 1881, 17.4 percent of the population over five could read and write a language, only 3.1 percent of whom were females. Between 1921 and 1946 the rate of literacy rose from 39.9 percent to 57.8 percent. In 1953 the rate was 64.7 percent, the average between a 75.9 percent male literacy and a 53.6 percent female literacy. By 1957 the rate had reached 70 percent.

This remarkable record has been achieved through an expanding, enlightened educational program. Under the British many schools were opened, and the desire of the Ceylonese to improve their status through education was encouraged. In 1943, education from kindergarten to university was declared free. All but a few private schools joined the free education scheme, under which the government pays the salaries of teachers and makes grants for equipment and maintenance. In 1956, there were 3,735 Government Schools and 3,131 Assisted Schools. All these schools are required by law to admit pupils irrespective of race, nationality, or religion.

School attendance is compulsory between the ages of five and fourteen except where there are no schools within a reasonable distance of the student's place of residence. The number of schools is still not adequate to take care of the growing population, and a smaller proportion of school-age children are in school than the generous law would indicate. The Ministry of Education controls this ambitious program under a Director of Education, aided by Local Advisory Committees. In 1956, expenditures for education were nearly Rs. 160 million ($33.7 million), about 11.5 percent of the national budgetary expenditure. This represented an increase of about Rs. 55 million (almost $11.6 million) over 1950.

The emphasis in most schools is on such general cultural subjects as reading, writing, history, geography, mathematics, language, art, music, and religion, though some vocational subjects like carpentry, lacquer work, and leather work are also taught. The primary grades go through the Eighth Standard, about age fourteen. At that point, according to a ruling that was supposed to take effect in 1956, students are subjected

57

to fitness tests. Those who pass are permitted to continue in free secondary schools, completing their studies at about age nineteen. Those who fail are supposed to be shifted to free vocational schools. The Eighth Standard fitness test, bitterly opposed by many parents, who felt that too much of a child's future would be determined by the results of an examination at too early an age, has never actually been held. It was suspended before the date of its first trial, "pending the provision of facilities for those who will be rejected as unfit for further academic education," according to the official Government Year Book. The facilities had not yet been provided in 1959. This attention to vocational training is an attempt to remedy the academic character of the education developed under the British, which bore little relation to what an early government report called "the practical aspects of life." One of the great problems of Ceylon is that too many men have been educated as clerks for whom there are no jobs, and too few as technicians for whom there is great need.

The University of Ceylon is located on one of the most beautiful campuses in the world, in Peradeniya, not far from Kandy, a short distance from the magnificent Botanical Gardens. It was established in 1942 by the incorporation of the Ceylon University College, founded in 1921, which prepared for the external degrees of the University of London, and the Ceylon

Medical College, founded in 1870. It is legally autonomous, though it receives an annual grant from the government. The University offers courses in Oriental Studies, Liberal Arts, Education, Law, Science, Agriculture, Medicine, Veterinary Science, and Engineering. The number of students in 1956 was 2,534, studying for thirteen different degrees, including the Ph.D. and M.D.

In addition to the Law Faculty of the University, there is a Law College for the legal education of students who want to qualify as Advocates and Proctors of the Supreme Court. The Ceylon Technical College provides training in engineering, vocational studies, and commerce. Only its engineering department is at university level, preparing for the examinations leading to the external degree of Bachelor of Science in Engineering of the University of London. Students may study for other examinations given under the rigorous supervision of the University of London without attending classes in any institution, working under tutors, or they may enroll in the collegiate departments of Jaffna College, an American-sponsored missionary school founded in 1828, or Aquinas University, a Catholic school in Colombo. There are also a number of teacher-training schools, none qualified to grant degrees. Two *Pirivenas,* schools for the training of Buddhist *bhikkus,* were given legal university status on January 1, 1959: Vidyalankara University and

59

Vidyodaya University, both located within a few miles of Colombo.

Ceylon's schools, hopefully attempting to cut down the illiteracy that still keeps a third of the population ignorant, have been caught in the grim struggle over languages. National pride now insists that English be at best a second language, requiring instruction in Sinhalese and Tamil throughout the school system, even though few textbooks, especially in technical subjects, are yet available. The *Swabhasha* or local-language schedule originally laid down included the high schools as of January 1, 1959, allowing discretion in the use of the three languages in certain subjects, among them mathematics, the sciences, and economics. The Tamils, whose language is spoken by some fifty million south Indians, are luckier than the Sinhalese since they may import books from India, but the Sinhalese must start from scratch. The fine boys' preparatory schools, like Royal College and St. Thomas's, in Colombo, in which many leaders in government and the professions have studied, equipping them well for the British universities that many of them have attended, have in the past maintained high standards of English instruction. The deterioration of English in these and other schools is bound to cause difficulty at the university level, which has not yet shifted to the local languages. It is unlikely that any considerable part of the bibliography essential in modern higher education will be translated into Sinhalese for many years to come. The loss of English, not only as an international medium of communication in which the English-trained leaders of Ceylon's independence excelled, but as a common language for the Tamils and Sinhalese who do not understand each other's speech, is a significant part of the evolution of modern Ceylon.

3. History in Legend and Fact

The Legends

The legendary history of Ceylon goes back to the
time of the events pictured in the great Sanskrit epic,
The Ramayana, supposedly 3000 B.C. *The Ramayana,*
a long poem thought to have been written by an Indian
poet named Valmiki, who lived about 500 B.C., tells
about the conquest of Ceylon by Rama, an incarnation
of the Hindu god, Vishnu. The story of Rama's rescue
of his beautiful wife, held prisoner in Ceylon, is delightful enough to be told for its own sake, without
reference to the interpretation that Rama's victory
over the demon hordes of Lanka symbolized the
spread southward to Ceylon of Brahmanic civilization.

Rama, the seventh incarnation of Vishnu, was the

virtuous and brave son of a north Indian king. Shortly before he was to succeed his aging father to the throne, his stepmother asked the king for a favor. Thinking his young wife wanted a present or leave to visit relatives, the old man promised the favor before he knew what it was. The scheming stepmother, taking advantage of the king's pledged word, demanded that Rama be sent into exile for fourteen years and that her son, Bharata, Rama's half-brother, be made king. Under the fatalistic Hindu system, Rama obediently accepted the consequences of his father's foolish promise and took his beautiful wife Sita and another half-brother, Lakshmana, into the jungles of south India. Everybody was miserable, including Bharata, who had no desire to be king, calling his mother a selfish, cruel woman. He even visited Rama in the jungle and urged him to come home. But Rama considered himself bound to honor his father's word.

One day, when Rama and Lakshmana were away from the cave in which they lived, the demon king of Lanka, a ten-headed monster named Ravana, dropped down in an early version of the flying-machine and carried off Sita to his castle in the mountains of south-central Ceylon. Rama, assisted by an army of monkeys, under the inspired leadership of the monkey chief, Hanuman, built a bridge of boulders across the Palk Strait (the legendary explanation for the formation now called Adam's Bridge, clearly visible from the air

63

as a barely submerged series of shallows), and invaded Lanka. After many bloody battles with Ravana's demon soldiers, Rama and Hanuman finally killed Ravana and rescued Sita, who had successfully resisted Ravana's advances. The victory coincided with the end of Rama's fourteen years of exile, and Rama took his wife and Hanuman back home to India and became king. Rama and Sita are worshiped today by devout Hindus, invariably accompanied by their friend Hanuman, the popular monkey-god. Two places, Sitawaka (now called Avisawella), thirty-six miles east of Colombo, and Sita Eliya, near Nuwara Eliya, high in the mountains about a hundred miles over winding roads from Colombo, commemorate the prison fortress of Sita. Her name is a popular first name of Ceylonese girls, both Sinhalese and Tamil.

A second legend about Ceylon's distant past tells about another cruel king named Suran, a tyrant with supernatural power. His people cried out to heaven in protest against his oppression. One of the gods, Skanda, also called Subrahmanya, one of the two sons of Siva, came down and drove Suran from his capital in southern Ceylon into the mountains, freeing the people. There is a famous temple dedicated to Skanda at Kataragama, in the jungle of southeastern Ceylon, to which come many pilgrims, both Buddhist and Hindu.

Other stories about ancient Ceylon, before the time of Vijaya, have no more evidence to support them than the legends of Sita and Skanda—indeed not as much, since no village-names or temples celebrate them. One is that a colony of Tamils from south India occupied what is now Trincomalee, on the east coast, as long ago as the 26th century B.C., about the time that the Hittites began to gain power in Asia Minor. Another is that Ceylon was part of an island continent which reached all the way east to Sumatra and Malaya and west to Madagascar, but which was separated from India (modern scholars say that Ceylon is geologically part of India, though some species of Ceylon fauna may be found in Sumatra and not in India). Ravana's demons stayed on in another bit of folk-lore as the Yakkhas or Rakshas, who were the principal residents of Ceylon when Vijaya arrived. The Yakkhas were no doubt devil worshipers rather than demons themselves. Some of them were assimilated with the Sinhalese invaders; others, avoiding contact, took refuge in the deep jungles. Their descendants are called Veddahs. Ethnologically they are related to the Semang or Pangan of the Malay Peninsula and the Andaman Islands. One of *their* stories is that Ceylon was once peopled by men with tails who climbed trees like monkeys. They were, perhaps, Hanuman's followers who mated with the widows of Ravana's soldiers and stayed behind to colonize Lanka. At the time of

Vijaya's arrival a tribe of snake-worshipers, the Nagas, also inhabited the interior of Lanka.

The Mahavamsa

The first recorded history of Ceylon is the remarkable epic chronicle of the Sinhalese kings, *The Mahavamsa*. It was written in Pali by Buddhist priests under the editorship of a monk named Mahanama in the fifth century A.D., on the leaves of the talipot palm. The old method of writing, using a stylus steadied in a notch in the thumb-nail of the scribe, may still be seen in Buddhist temples and *viharas* (monasteries). The incised leaves, over which a powder was dusted to make the words stand out, were bound together between board covers. Thousands of these *ola* manuscripts lie in temple libraries, where they are studied by the monks. *The Mahavamsa* was an adaptation in stately language of an earlier, cruder version of the chronicle, *The Dipavamsa,* written in the fourth century A.D. *The Mahavamsa,* which means "Great Dynasty," ends with the death of King Mahasena in 352 A.D. The account of the later kings, called *The Culavamsa,* "Lesser Dynasty," was continued by Buddhist monks at various times after the thirteenth century, taking the story down through the last of the Kandyan rulers, Sri Wickrama Rajasinha, who was deposed by the British in 1815.

According to *The Mahavamsa* (whose translation

into English by Wilhelm Geiger was first published in 1912), Vijaya, a prince of western India from what is now Gujerat, of Bengali descent, founder of the Sinhalese race, landed in Ceylon on the same day that Buddha attained Nirvana. That date is usually reckoned by the Sinhalese as 543 B.C., though Geiger argues that the time of Vijaya's arrival was in 483 B.C., the year now generally accepted as that of Gautama Buddha's death. Vijaya was evidently an undisciplined young man in his native Gujerat, where he and his friends committed "many intolerable deeds of violence." Banished by his father with seven hundred followers, Vijaya was put on a ship, which eventually landed on the island of Lanka, "in the region called Tambapanni." No one knows where Tambapanni was, for the "red earth" could have been on either the east or west coast. The ships of the 5th century B.C. must have been much larger and more seaworthy than the fragile catamarans which sail between India and Ceylon today.

Vijaya

Vijaya's first experience in Ceylon was very like that of Ulysses on the island of Circe as he returned from the Trojan War (just as Rama's rescue of Sita has a literary parallel in the kidnaping and recovery of Helen after a bloody war on the plains of Troy). On their arrival, Vijaya's company, exploring the new

land, was put under a spell by a Yakkha princess
named Kuvanna, who was a sorceress. Vijaya, when
they did not return, took up the five traditional weapons: sword, bow, battle-axe, spear, and shield, went
after the Indian Ocean Circe, and threatened to kill
her if she did not immediately free his men. Impressed by his manliness, she said, "Spare my life, sir,
and I will give thee a kingdom and do thee a woman's
service and other service as thou wilt."

Vijaya, who had no Penelope waiting for him, saw
that the princess, in spite of her witchcraft, was attractive, arranged for the release of his men, and
then "took her to him as his spouse and lay with her
blissfully" on a splendid, canopied bed which she
materialized by means of her magic. During the night
they heard music, which the princess told Vijaya came
from a great gathering of Yakkhas celebrating a royal
wedding. Not a girl to enter an affair half-heartedly,
she advised him to take advantage of the festival, for
which a great multitude had gathered, and destroy
the Yakkhas. Without delay, Vijaya summoned his
men and fell upon the marriage party. After killing all
the Yakkhas, he put on the garments of the Yakkha
king and set up the first Sinhalese monarchy.

When his chief officers had founded villages, mainly
in the neighborhood of the future capital of Ceylon,
Anuradhapura, and established their rule over the
local tribes, they asked Vijaya to be consecrated as

king. He refused until a suitable queen might be procured for him, having grown weary of Kuvanna, who had borne him a son and a daughter. Envoys were sent to what is now Madura, in southeastern India, to persuade the daughter of the king to come to Lanka to be Vijaya's queen. The mission was eminently successful, not only discovering a suitable royal wife for Vijaya but nearly a hundred other lovely Tamil maidens for the ministers and retainers of Vijaya's court. We may assume that during the two years or so of Vijaya's consolidation of his new kingdom, they had followed his example and temporarily comforted themselves with the local girls.

Poor Kuvanna, banished by Vijaya, who told her that she had to go because his men were afraid of witches, went back to her own people, and was put to death. The children were taken to Adam's Peak by an uncle, where eventually the brother married his sister. They became, according to *The Mahavamsa,* the ancestors of the Veddahs.

Meanwhile, Vijaya and his bride were consecrated king and queen in a solemn ceremony. The most favored followers received their wives according to rank. The new Sinhalese dynasty, with an early admixture of Tamil blood, was in full swing. Vijaya, in the words of the chronicler, forsaking his former evil ways, ruled over all Lanka as lord of men, in peace and righteousness, for thirty-eight years.

This candid account of Vijaya's strenuous first years in Ceylon, says the scribe, was "compiled for the serene joy and emotion of the pious."

The Coming of Buddhism

For nearly two hundred years the kingdom of the Sinhala, as Vijaya had decided to call his people, in honor of his father, the son of a lion, was so occupied with colonization from India, road-building, and irrigation projects against the seasonal droughts, that not much attention was paid to religion. Vijaya concentrated his efforts on agricultural development, inviting merchants and farmers from India to take possession of the rich and fertile land. Buddhism had already become firmly established in India, the birthplace of Gautama Buddha in the 6th century B.C. Vijaya himself seems to have been a Hindu Brahman, though some of his followers were probably Buddhists. Yet no mention is made of any religious activity on their part, and Vijaya's immediate successors gave equal respect to Yakkha temples, halls built for the worshipers of Brahma, and even to what *The Mahavamsa* calls heretical beliefs.

During the reign of Devanampiya Tissa (307–267 B.C.), Mahinda, the son of the great Buddhist king of India, Asoka, came to convert the island of Lanka. *The Mahavamsa* tells how Mahinda "rose up in the air" from a Buddhist monastery in India and descended upon the hill of Mihintale, not far from Anuradhapura in Ceylon. King Tissa, who had arranged a big hunting party on that day, went to Mihintale with forty thousand of his men. The god of the mountain, who wanted to bring Tissa and Mahinda together, appeared in the form of a *sambhur* (Ceylon elk), browsing in the thicket. The king, a fine sportsman, was unwilling to kill an unheeding creature and so twanged his bow-string to warn the animal. As the stag fled, Tissa pursued him. When they came near Mahinda, the stag vanished, and the Buddhist saint and the Sinhalese king stood face to face. As a result of this meeting Tissa was converted to Buddhism, which spread rapidly throughout Lanka. It took such firm root that it is today the vital faith of most of the Sinhalese people, many centuries after it all but disappeared in India.

On the top of the rocky hill of Mihintale, a thousand feet above the plain a *vihara* or monastery was built to commemorate the conversion of King Tissa. In time the holy mountain was covered with shrines and temples, the ruins of which may still be seen. On the eastern side a giant stairway of 1,840 steps, made from slabs of granite (with the exception of the last 150 steps, which are carved from the living rock), leads to the summit of Mihintale. The steps have been deeply worn by hundreds of thousands of barefooted pilgrims who climb each year to the place where Buddhism was born in Ceylon. In the Ambastala *Dagoba,* the typical bell-shaped shrine of Ceylon, are the ashes of Mahinda, who spent the rest of his life on the spot where he and Tissa had met.

As the followers of Tissa became Buddhist, many of them assumed the robes of monks. No women were permitted to be ascetics, however, because there was no qualified priestess to accept their vows. Mahinda therefore sent for his sister Sanghamitta, the prioress of a Buddhist convent in India. He also asked his sister to request permission of their father Asoka to bring back with her a branch of the sacred Bo-tree (in India called the pipul, of the fig family), under which Buddha attained his Buddhahood. Asoka agreed and presided over a ceremony during which a branch of the Bo-tree, self-severed, rooted itself in a golden vase, which Asoka had had made. It was transported by Sanghamitta to Ceylon, where it was planted in Anuradhapura. From it miraculously grew eight shoots, which were planted in various parts of Ceylon, becoming the progenitors of the thousands of Bo-trees in the island today, all deeply revered by devout Buddhists. What is believed to be the parent tree, said to be the oldest living thing in the world, still grows among the noble ruins of Anuradhapura after twenty-two centuries. It may be seen by visitors to Ceylon today, its gnarled branches hung with bits of white cloth, tokens of reverence placed there by the faithful, its heart-shaped leaves trembling in the lightest breeze.

The importance of Buddhism to Ceylon, which became a spiritual center of Hinayana Buddhism, cannot be overestimated. For example, *The Mahavamsa,* the principal source of our knowledge of early Ceylonese history, was written as a glorification of the Buddhist religion, not as a comprehensive chronicle of events. The "great" period which the title refers to is that during which the kings built *dagobas* and *viharas* and gave generous gifts to the *bhikkus* or monks. After 300 A.D., the priestly chroniclers felt that the record of the heresies that crept into Buddhist worship, the Tamil invasions, and the general decline in the importance of the *bhikkus* deserved no better name than *Culuvamsa,* the lower or lesser dynasty. Nevertheless, the piety of the kings was a vital factor in holding the Sinhalese people together in the face of powerful threats by the Hindus of south India, the Catholic Portuguese, and the Protestant Dutch and English. Among the most remarkable archaeological remains on the island today are the bell- and dome-shaped *dagobas* (sometimes called *stupas*) in which were preserved relics of Lord Buddha. Some of these shrines, together with splendid statues of Buddha and religious frescoes, are among the world's art treasures. Still more important was the influence on the religious faith of countless millions of other Asians, who were

73

converted to Buddhism by Ceylonese and Indian missionaries. In Ceylon too the vast scholarship of Buddhism, of which *The Dipavamsa, The Mahavamsa, The Culavamsa,* and the books of Buddha's teachings are examples, was concentrated.

Dutthagamini

The Sinhalese kings, struggling against invaders and usurpers, moving their capital many times as foreign conquerors took over portions of the island, kept their succession clear (though some of the kings were Tamils) down to the beginning of the nineteenth century, one of the longest dynasties on record. Most of what occurred during their reigns worthy of preservation, whether in the arts or agriculture, was accomplished in the name of Buddhism. For example, during the reign of the great king Dutthagamini (161–137 B.C.) was built a remarkable palace for the priests of the many temples of the sacred city of Anuradhapura, nine stories high, one hundred fifty feet square, containing "a thousand well-arranged chambers . . . overlaid with various gems and adorned with windows," as *The Mahavamsa* describes it. The sixteen hundred monolithic columns of granite, each twelve feet high, on which this enormous building rested, may be seen among the ruins of Anuradhapura, all that is left of the mighty "Brazen Palace," so called because it was roofed with brazen tiles. The tanks or "consecrated

74

lakes" for water storage which are among the marvels of early engineering, were invariably built in the name of Buddha. The oldest architectural monument now extant in either India or Ceylon is the tremendous *dagoba* called the Abhayagiriya, built by King Vattagamini between 88 and 76 B.C.

The dynastic history of Ceylon is too complex to be very interesting outside the island except to scholars. Of the sixty-one kings listed in *The Mahavamsa,* a few, particularly the nationally popular Dutthagamini, stand out as heroes of the people, whose names are remembered with respect and affection by present-day Ceylonese. Some of their stories are well worth re-telling.

Among the sixty-one, which include a number of the Indian conquerors, was one woman, Anula, a Sinhalese Messalina. She poisoned her first husband, a wicked king who seems to have deserved his fate. One of his palace guards became king and married Anula, who hurried him along to his next incarnation because she had become enamored of a Tamil carpenter. The carpenter then married Anula and shared her throne until she fell in love with a wood-carrier. He lasted a little over a year before she decided that a Brahman palace-priest would be a more satisfying husband and king. Meanwhile, Anula, according to *The Mahavamsa,* became romantically interested in a number of her palace guards. After poisoning the

Brahman, Anula reigned alone for four months, attended by the guardsmen. Finally she was killed by the son of an earlier king.

There is no other evidence of royal villainy in *The Mahavamsa*. The early kings of Ceylon, both Sinhalese and Tamil, seem to have been virtuous men, notable for their good works and piety, though their reigns were generally uneventful.

The story of Dutthagamini and his predecessor, Elara, however, would be interesting in any nation's history. In 205 B.C. a Tamil of noble descent, Elara, came to the throne of Lanka, one of four south Indian invaders who ruled Ceylon between 237 and 161 B.C. Elara was famous as a just king who had a bell hung at the head of his bed with a long rope so that anyone who wanted a judgment at law might ring it at any time. On one occasion the king's only son accidentally ran over a calf with his bullock-cart, killing it. When the mother cow came and pulled the rope, Elara, honoring her appeal, ordered his son executed. Another story told of Elara's conscientious rule is about an old woman who spread out some rice to dry in the sun. Suddenly an unseasonable rain came, ruining the rice. The old woman went to the palace and pulled Elara's bell. Elara took under advisement her claim that the rain had no business falling at that time. He reasoned that "a king who observes justice surely obtains rain in due season." His prayers were heard by the gods of the four quarters of the world, high in the Hindu pantheon, and during the rest of his rule no rain fell during the daytime. It rained only at night, once a week, in sufficient abundance that cisterns were constantly filled.

At this time, in Kelaniya, a short distance north of modern Colombo, visited by Lord Buddha on one of his three journeys to Ceylon, a Sinhalese of royal descent was king, paying annual tribute to Elara, King of Anuradhapura and Overlord of all Lanka. The daughter of the king, the beautiful princess Devi, was put to sea in an open boat as a sacrifice to the god of the sea who had devastated the coast with floods. Her boat was driven ashore in southern Ceylon in the sub-kingdom of Ruhuna. Soon the king, Kavan Tissa, made her his queen. When she became pregnant, she craved three extraordinary things: to have a huge honey-comb, whose honey she wanted to distribute to many *bhikkus;* to drink the water in which the sword used to cut off the head of King Elara's chief general had been washed, and to stand on the severed head; and to adorn herself with garlands of lotus brought from the enemy capital of Anuradhapura. The royal astrologers, consulted about the meaning of her wishes declared that she would be the mother of a noble king who would defeat the Tamils and bring honor to the holy cause of Buddhism. Queen Devi's desires were granted, with some difficulty, and in time she became the mother of a son, who was named Gamini. Two years later, without the help of omens, another son, Tissa, was born. From early childhood the two boys were pledged to hatred of the Tamil invaders of their country.

When Gamini was sixteen years old, his father set him up in his own establishment, to which was soon attracted a band of ten great warriors famous for their strength and courage. They formed a sort of Sinhalese Round Table, the names of whose members, according to the Sinhalese writer, John M. Seneveratna, "among the most glorious in Ceylon history, are still today, over two thousand years later, household words among the Sinhalese throughout the length and breadth of Lanka."

Each of the ten Paladins or Giants had some unusual talent. For example, Nandhimitti was immensely strong. The son of a Sinhalese general in Elara's army, he was angered because the Tamils desecrated his offerings at the sacred Bo-tree in Anuradhapura. He killed as many of them as he could, tearing them in two, and then fled to the south to help Gamini fight for Buddhism. Another Paladin, Bharana, was so fleet of foot that he amused himself by running down rabbits, *sambhurs,* and boars. Phusadena was the greatest marksman of his day. He was able to shoot an arrow through a wagon loaded with sand and a hundred skins or through wood sixteen inches thick.

Velusumana was the greatest horseman of his time. And so on. Gamini and Tissa spent most of their days in military exercises with these gifted warriors. Gamini became an excellent swordsman and rider of both elephants and horses.

In time King Kavan Tissa called together an army to march against the Tamils, equipping it with elephants, horse-drawn chariots, and weapons. Prince Gamini, appointed Commander-in-Chief, was all for immediately attacking Elara's army, but his father felt that the time was not yet ripe. Gamini defied the king's orders and demanded permission to enter the Tamil territory. Kavan Tissa pointed out that Elara had over a million soldiers, against a much smaller Sinhalese army. Gamini insisted, calling his father a coward. Kavan Tissa angrily ordered his son's arrest, but Gamini ran away from his troops and went into hiding. From that time he was known as Dutthagamini, which in Sinhalese means "the undutiful Gamini." Not long afterward King Kavan Tissa died, having made the Ten Paladins swear that they would not take sides in any contest between his two sons.

Before the funeral rites were over, there was trouble. Dutthagamini was made king, but his brother Tissa gathered an army and refused to acknowledge Dutthagamini's authority. The new king thereupon marched against Tissa, thinking to force him to give up their mother and Dutthagamini's favorite elephant,

Kandula (as famous in Ceylon as Robert E. Lee's horse, Traveller, is in American history). Their first meeting in battle resulted in victory for Tissa, and Dutthagamini had to flee to escape capture. He quickly assembled a new army, however, and once more faced Tissa's troops. Realizing that further civil war among the Sinhalese would postpone the much more important program of getting rid of Elara and his Tamils, Dutthagamini challenged Tissa to single combat.

The challenge was accepted, and the two fighting brothers met between their armies. It was a strange match: Dutthagamini was mounted on a horse, Tissa on the stolen Kandula. They circled about each other, Tissa leaning far over the side of his elephant to strike whenever Dutthagamini came close enough. Dutthagamini, anxious to hurt neither his brother nor Kandula, born the same day as himself, settled the duel in an ingenious way. Pulling his mare back on her haunches, he suddenly urged her forward, leaping all the way over Kandula. As he passed, Dutthagamini swung his sword downward, inflicting a wound on Kandula's back. The elephant, frightened by the flying mare and maddened with pain, bucked off his rider and headed for home. That was the end of the battle. Tissa took refuge in a *vihara,* but soon made his peace with Dutthagamini and was loyal to him from that time forward.

80

Now Dutthagamini began serious preparation for his war against Elara. Leaving Tissa behind to look after his people and take care of the crops, Dutthagamini started north with an army which *The Maha-vamsa* says stretched out for some thirty-five miles. Crossing the great river of Ceylon, the Mahaveli-ganga, which marked the boundary between Tamil-land and the land of the Sinhalese, Dutthagamini sub-dued one Tamil stronghold after another. He was held up for several months while his army besieged the most important fort in the defenses of Anuradhapura, the city of Vijita, which was surrounded by three moats and protected by a high wall, whose four gates were made of wrought iron. The Ten Paladins and Kandula figured bravely in the attack. Kandula, whose task was to batter down the South Gate, was repulsed with balls of red-hot iron and molten pitch, but returned in copper armor to knock down the gate so that the Paladins and the army could enter and defeat the Tamils.

The final battle was fought about eighteen miles southeast of Anuradhapura, at Khagalagama. There Dutthagamini entrenched his army and waited for Elara to attack. The Tamil army was led by Elara himself, mounted on his favorite elephant Mahapab-bata, surrounded by a picked bodyguard of twenty warriors. Dutthagamini took his place at the center of his troops, his Pearl Parasol above him as a sign of royalty. At first the fight went against the Sinhalese, raging most furiously around the center of the line commanded by Dutthagamini. Then, after the champion warrior of the Tamils, Dighajantu, was killed by Suranimila, the heaviest drinker among the Paladins (his name means alcoholic spirits), the Tamils were disastrously routed.

Elara escaped, but Dutthagamini caught up with him near the south gate of Anuradhapura. There they fought in single combat, mounted on their elephants. Elara, tired and discouraged by the defeat of his army, was no match for Dutthagamini, who easily evaded the dart thrown at him and made Kandula charge Elara's elephant. As Kandula's tusks gored Mahapabbata, Dutthagamini threw his javelin, mortally wounding Elara. Dutthagamini, a good winner, gave Elara an honorable funeral as a brave man and just ruler. Elara was cremated where he died, and Dutthagamini had erected in his memory a splendid monument, on which was a sign, "Let no man, prince or peasant, in future pass this way riding in palanquin or litter, or with beating of drums." For more than two thousand years that order was obeyed.

Under the rule of the noble King Dutthagamini, which lasted for twenty-four years, the Sinhalese people prospered. In their capital city of Anuradhapura were built many shrines and temples, some of whose ruins will be described in a later chapter. It was a time of honor for Buddhism and of great cultural development.

The story of Dutthagamini, including the account of the construction of the *dagobas,* takes up eleven of the thirty-seven chapters of *The Mahavamsa*. It is typical of the kind of heroic story celebrated in Sinhalese art, drama, and literature down to the present day.

Kasyapa

Under many of the sixty-two kings who followed the *Mahavamsa* period Hinduism influenced and weakened Buddhism. For several hundred years, indeed, Ceylon was little more than a dependency of the Chola Kingdom in south India. The preoccupation with religion of the writer-monks, who kept the principal records we have of the centuries before the coming of the Portuguese, tended to bias their accounts. It is far from true that there were no great leaders during this period besides Parakrama Bahu the Great, first after Dutthagamini in the hearts of his countrymen. For example, one king was a skilful physician who worked for the health of his people, building hospitals and personally attending to the sick. He even introduced a kind of veterinary service into the island. Under several of the kings the arts flourished, and the magnificent frescoes still to be seen in the shrines and on the rocky walls of caves at Dambulla and at Sigiriya were painted. Jettha Tissa, in the fourth century A.D., was himself an artist—a painter, sculptor, and carver of ivory—who founded schools of art and served as patron for other artists. In the sixth century King Kumara Dhatusena was a well-known poet.

King Kasyapa, who seized the throne from his father in 479 A.D., is the most notorious villain of Ceylonese history. The antithesis of the gallant, pious Dutthagamini, he is the symbol of everything the Sinhalese despise: cowardice, cruelty, sensuality. The story of Kasyapa, associated with the superb rock fortress of Sigiriya, is a fascinating one, for Kasyapa, a thoroughly bad sort, is, like most scoundrel-heroes of literature, a romantic figure.

Kasyapa's father, Dhatu Sena, was a good man who had lived in exile during the reign of five Tamil usurpers. His teacher was the monk Mahanama, author-editor of *The Mahavamsa*. As a young man he had entered the Buddhist priesthood, but gave up a life of contemplation to make war against the Tamils. Successful, he devoted himself to the arts of peace, founding hospitals, building tanks, establishing monasteries, using his personal store of jewels to replace those that had been stolen from sacred statues by looters. He had two sons, Kasyapa and Moggallana.

Kasyapa, jealous of what he thought was his father's preference for his younger brother, forced Moggallana to take refuge in India and threw the old king into prison. Then he ordered guards to put his father to death by stripping him, binding him with chains, and walling up the entrance to his cell. Finally, fearing the disapproval of his people and the vengeance of Moggallana, he moved his capital from Anuradhapura to the mighty rock of Sigiriya, about sixty miles to the southeast. There it stands alone in the plain, a rough mass of granite twice as long as it is wide, over four hundred feet high, the highest part overhanging the steep sides. Around the base of the great rock he built a walled city, surrounded by a moat. Part of the moat, now covered with lotus, still forms a beautiful pond, in which Sigiriya, the "Lion-Rock," is reflected.

By a remarkable feat of engineering, Kasyapa's men constructed a gallery, protected by a nine-foot wall, winding up to the overhang on the top. There, from between the carved forepaws of a lion, whose body must be imagined as the rock itself, steps were built past the overhang, and from there to the top, cut out of the rock itself. The ascent of Sigiriya past the gallery is frightening even today, though metal guard rails have been put up to keep visitors from being blown off. On top of Sigiriya Kasyapa built a palace, baths, a reservoir, houses for his retainers, even a formal garden. In this impregnable fortress he spent eighteen miserable years, repenting his sins and keeping a sharp eye out for his brother, who was rumored to be gathering an army in India to come back and avenge his father.

In his remorse Kasyapa became very religious, filling his walled city with temples, hospitals, almshouses, and other public buildings, and giving lavishly to the Buddhist priests who lived within the walls. Night after night his guards kept watch, waiting for Moggallana to attack, though no army equipped with the weapons of that time could have carried Sigiriya by force. Kasyapa must have stored vast supplies of food, knowing that only a long siege could hurt him. During those long watches a talented soldier—or perhaps a bored member of the royal household—whiled away the time by painting on the walls of Sigiriya. Almost fifteen hundred years later, in a shallow indentation of the rock, forty feet above the gallery, some of the frescoes, exposed to the weather all those hundreds of years, still hold their glowing colors. The Sigiriya frescoes, which are generally recognized as among the important works of art from the past, will be described in a later chapter.

When Moggallana finally came, Kasyapa panicked. Instead of roosting safely on his high rock, whose approaches could have been defended by a handful of men, he led his army outside the moat and the wall to meet his brother's army of Indian mercenaries on the open plain. His men chased a small force of Indians southwest about fifty miles near what is now Kurunegala. There they found the main body of Moggallana's troops waiting for them. In the violent battle that followed, Kasyapa at first had the advantage. Hopefully, he pressed on to end the dread that had tormented him ever since he had killed his father. His elephant, however, refused to cross a marsh that stretched between him and Moggallana. As he turned back to find a way around the marsh, his men, thinking that he was retreating, broke in dosorder. Their hearts may not have been in the battle for which they had prepared so long. The wonder is that the psychotic king, hated by most of the Sinhalese people, had an army at all. In any event, Moggallana quickly caught up with his forsaken brother and put an end to him. Another version of the story is that Kasyapa forced his elephant to enter the swamp, where it sank to its belly in the mud. When he saw that he would be captured by Moggallana, Kasyapa committed suicide under the feet of his own elephant.

Between Anuradhapura and Polonnaruwa

The chronological pattern is now clear: there was perpetual struggle against Indian usurpers, who often won and made vassals of the Sinhalese nobility. In the periods of peace *dagobas* and other religious buildings were erected, the magnificent network of irrigation tanks was added to, the dams breached by the invaders were repaired, roads were built, and works of art were completed. By the end of the sixth century A.D. the most notable feature of the country was the system of tanks. Outside of the splendid capital of Anuradhapura there were few cities. The trade of the day was mostly in the hands of foreign merchants, many of them from Egypt. At one time small Roman copper coins of the fourth century were the principal currency in Ceylon. Williams mentions that during the excavations at Sigiriya some sixteen hundred coins were found, all but twelve of them Roman. The chief port of the day was in the northwest, at Mantota, at the base of Mannar Island.

The weary succession of murder, civil war, invasion, and rebellion continued, with now and then a ruler from one of the south Indian kingdoms, Pandya and Chola, taking over the capital, only to be routed by the Sinhalese. The capital itself was shifted back and forth from Anuradhapura, which was often sacked, to Polonnaruwa, about sixty miles to the east. In 1017 A.D. the renowned Chola emperor, Rajaraja I, conquered the whole of Ceylon except in the most remote sections of the south, and the island became a province of the Chola empire. The capital, at Polonnaruwa, which was renamed Jananathapura, became a center of Hindu culture. Trade began to be dominated by Muslim merchants, first known in Ceylon in the early eighth century. During the twelfth and thirteenth centuries, while the country was still in the hands of the Chola kings, the Muslims had great commercial and, through influence in south India, political power. Chinese traders too were frequent visitors from the tenth to the thirteenth centuries.

Parakrama Bahu the Great

For a brief time the tide of south Indian power was rolled back under the benevolent rule of the most vigorous of Sinhalese kings, Parakrama Bahu the Great, who held off both the Indians and rival Sinhalese chieftains and made Polonnaruwa a brilliant capital. Parakrama Bahu was king from 1157 to 1186. During his reign he not only settled disputes among his own people which grew out of heresies among the Buddhists, but decisively defeated foreign enemies. Early in his reign Parakrama Bahu declared war on Burma, sending a fleet from Trincomalee during the southwest monsoon and landing in the kingdom of Pegu, in southern Burma. The cause of the war was disputes over the elephant trade, the rude treatment of Sinhalese ambassadors, and the seizure of a princess from Ceylon on her way to Cambodia. The king of Pegu was killed, and Burma for a time fell into Ceylon's orbit. Later Parakrama Bahu sent a Sinhalese army to the Chola kingdom and defeated the traditional enemies of his country. Reversing the familiar order, the Cholas paid tribute to Ceylon. Thus Parakrama established the first and only Ceylonese empire. It did not long survive him.

Parakrama Bahu was not only a successful military

leader but a tolerant and wise administrator. He solved religious problems by a far-sighted policy of preferring no one group to another, granting complete freedom of worship. Without destroying or desecrating the Hindu temples that had been built in Polonnaruwa, he built Buddhist shrines and *viharas* since he was himself a devout Buddhist. He also enlarged and fortified the city, building the usual places of worship, and also palaces, baths, schools, and gardens. Under him the magnificent system of irrigation tanks was at its height. Agriculture prospered, and everybody had plenty to eat. After Parakrama Bahu Ceylon declined, and for nearly eight hundred years was eclipsed by other nations.

Parakrama Bahu is the truly distinguished exemplar of the Sinhalese people, whose attainments under his leadership demonstrated vitality, initiative, and creative genius unsurpassed elsewhere in the world in the twelfth century. He is said to have been deeply versed in law, religion, medicine, logic, poetry, and music, as well as in the arts of war. His understanding of the importance of irrigation to his country indicates a very advanced concept of agriculture. In his first speech to his ministers, according to *The Culavamsa,* Parakrama said, "In a country like this not even the least quantity of rain water should be allowed to flow into the ocean without profiting man . . . Remember that it is not meet that men like unto us should live and enjoy what has come into our hands and care not for the people. Let there not be left anywhere in my kingdom a piece of land, though it be of the smallest dimensions, that does not yield some benefit to man."

Polonnaruwa was undoubtedly one of the magnificent capitals of the ancient world, not excepting Babylon, Cairo, and Athens. Tennent, who believed that at the time of Parakrama Ceylon had a population of over twenty million, estimated that Polonnaruwa was a city of three million inhabitants. It is doubtful, however, that the population of Ceylon was ever so large, though it must have had many more than the three and a half million to which it had shrunk in 1901. The many religious buildings, both Hindu and Buddhist, constructed during Parakrama's reign were colossal in the tradition of the Brazen Palace of Anuradhapura. Parakrama's *Dalada Maligawa,* as the Temple of Buddha's Tooth was called wherever the sacred relic was housed, was a superb stone building rather than the usual Sinhalese structure of bricks, with roofs, doors, and windows of gold and countless works of art both inside and outside. Parakrama's own palace was seven stories high and had a thousand rooms. Its roof had hundreds of pinnacles wrought in precious metals. In one of the massive Buddhist temples was a large granite seat on which was the following inscription, summarizing the achievements of Parakrama:

His Majesty Parakrama Bahu . . . , having made all Lanka's isle to appear like a festive island, having made all Lanka like unto a wishing-tree, having made all Lanka like unto an incomparably decorated house, having subjugated in war the Chola kings, went to India with great hosts. . . . Lanka having been neglected for a long time, he erected alms-houses at different places throughout South India and Ceylon; and on his return spent much treasure on mendicants. Not being content with all this, he determined on a distribution of alms four times in every year, and by giving gold, jewels, cloth, ornaments, etc., having extinguished the poverty of the inhabitants of the world, and done good to the world and to religion, this is the seat on which he sat to allay body weariness.

It is a pleasant thought that one of Ceylon's kings made all Lanka like unto a wishing-tree!

The Decline of the Sinhalese Kingdom

After the death of Parakrama in 1186 there were no more Sinhalese kings of note. South Indian invaders again became dominant, not only in the northern Kingdom of Pihiti, now called Jaffna, but in the southeastern stronghold of the Sinhalese, the Kingdom of Ruhuna. Twenty-nine years and fifteen kings after Parakrama, a fierce Malabar warrior named Magha invaded Ceylon and laid waste the splendid city of Polonnaruwa, persecuting the Buddhists and desecrating Buddhist temples. His troops, and those of his Tamil successors, more interested in loot than in development, did not look after the irrigation tanks, some five thousand in number at the time of Parakrama. The breached *bunds* or dams spilled the precious water into swamps in which malaria-carrying mosquitoes bred. The rich fields around Anuradhapura and Polonnaruwa eventually became parched and unproductive, and only those peasants too debilitated by malaria to go south stayed in what was to become the northern Dry Zone. The Tamils retreated to the Jaffna peninsula, where they established the Kingdom of Jaffna, more often than not a part of one or other of the south Indian kingdoms. The division of the Tamils in the north from the Sinhalese in the south, emphasizing differences in religion and language, has continued to this day, though many of both racial groups now live in other parts of the island.

The Sinhalese, withdrawing to the south, abandoned Polonnaruwa and established one capital after another as their kings were threatened by quarrelsome local leaders or by foreign invaders. At various times during the 13th, 14th, and 15th centuries, the Sinhalese kings were under the domination of the Pandyan and Chola kings, the Emperor of China, a Malayan king, and even for short periods the King of Pegu in Burma and the Sultan of Egypt. At one low point in the fortunes of the Sinhalese, the Pandyans captured the Tooth Relic and took it to India, from which it was recovered by the Sinhalese king only at the cost of his going to India in humble supplication and agreeing to Pandyan suzerainty. One of the weak Sinhalese kings of the 15th century, whose capital was at Gampaha in the Kandyan hills, was captured and carried off to China by a Chinese expedition which had been sent by the Emperor as a result of Ceylonese mistreatment of Chinese envoys. Three times between 1436 and 1459 the humiliated Sinhalese sent tribute to China.

During most of the century preceding the establishment of the Portuguese in 1505, the lowland Sinhalese capital of Ceylon was at Kotte, in a marshland near Colombo (which was then a settlement of foreign traders). Only in the highlands did the Sinhalese continue to hold out against foreign influence. The Kandyans, as the highland Sinhalese came to call themselves, were independent of both the Kotte dynasty and their various overlords. In the south were chaotically warring petty chieftains. Lanka, which had once proudly carried the power and culture of the Sinhalese to India and the Far East, had fallen on evil days. Her riches, which had long attracted merchants from many parts of the world, were at the mercy of the strongest exploiter.

The Portuguese Occupation

The Portuguese began their occupation of Ceylon on November 15, 1505, when Dom Lourenço de Almeida visited Colombo and carved the coat of arms of Portugal and the date 1501 on a rock, which may be seen today in a park near the harbor a few hundred yards from the spot where de Almeida landed. The date 1501 probably referred to an earlier visit by Portuguese to Galle. Dom Lourenço was escorted to Kotte, where the king bargained with him to take the lowland Sinhalese under the protection of Portugal in return for an annual tribute of cinnamon.

What King Vira Parakrama Bahu VIII wanted when he sought the protection of the Portuguese, whose armor and cannons impressed him very much, was security against the Moors in Colombo, the Tamils in Jaffna, and the warring Sinhalese princes in the highlands to the east and in many villages of the south. The Portuguese, gladly accepting the King's offer, built forts, first in Colombo and then in one city after another along the western coast, to help them compete for the spice trade with the hostile Moors. They governed from Goa, through a resident Captain General, who controlled the export of cinnamon, areca nuts, pepper, precious stones, and elephants.

Colombo and other coastal cities, including the prosperous port of Galle, had come under the control of the Moors, Muslim merchants and seamen, called Moors by the Portuguese as a generic word to describe any Muslims, regardless of their ethnic origin. Tennent says that they were descendants of Arab traders who came to Ceylon centuries before Mahomet was born, whose tough, energetic kinsmen built up remarkable commercial establishments throughout the East. The Moors, still conducting shrewd business in Ceylon today, trace their ancestry to those Middle Eastern traders who intermarried with the local women and converted them to Islam.

For 150 years the Portuguese held the coastal strip which produced most of Ceylon's fabulous wealth. It was not an easy time for them, for the highland Sinhalese bitterly resented the alliance between the kings of Kotte and the Portuguese, who put down the repeated raids by the Kandyans with fierce brutality. One brave young Sinhalese leader stands out in the sordid story of treachery and bloodshed that marked the ascendancy of the Portuguese in Ceylon. His name was Rajasinha I, King of Sitawaka, his capital from 1554 to 1593 in the foothills of central Ceylon's high mountains thirty-six miles east of Colombo. Rajasinha, whose name means "Lion King," besieged Kotte and drove the feeble lowland king, Dharmapala, who had been converted to Catholicism by the Portuguese, into Colombo. He defeated the Portuguese in open battle near Colombo and laid siege to Colombo many times, once so successfully that the defenders were forced to eat the flesh of their own casualties. Moving on to Kandy, he drove into exile the Kandyan king. An excellent organizer, he was able to assemble formidable armies and equip them with guns and even artillery, though gunpowder was not known in Ceylon until the arrival of the Portuguese. He even fitted out a small naval force and attacked the Portuguese from the sea as well as the land. At one point he was master of all Ceylon with the exception of Colombo and the Kingdom of Jaffna. Ironically, he was defeated by a rival Sinhalese king, not by the Portuguese. Though Rajasinha renounced Buddhism to become a Hindu and harshly treated the Buddhist priests who naturally disapproved of him, his brave and bold defense of Lanka against foreign invaders has endeared him to the Sinhalese.

In 1560 a Portuguese military mission captured the sacred Tooth Relic, which had been taken to Jaffna by one of its royal guardians, fleeing from both the Portuguese and the formidable Rajasinha. The King of Burma offered a large ransom for the Tooth, but the Portuguese, considering it a heathen fetish, sent it to Goa, where it was reportedly burned by the Portuguese Archbishop in the presence of the Viceroy.

The story of the Tooth Relic links the legendary history of Ceylon with the present. It is the one unvarying center of faith through good periods and through evil ones. From the time of its arrival in Ceylon, hidden in the hair of a princess from Orissa in northeastern India in 313 A.D. to the annual August *Perahera* or procession in honor of the Tooth Relic, it has been a unifying force for the Sinhalese.

The Sacred Tooth was found after the cremation of Gautama Buddha in 483 B.C. and kept for eight hundred years in what is now the Bihar Province of India before it was taken to Ceylon. Until it was allegedly destroyed by the Portuguese, it followed the fortunes of the Sinhalese kings from one *Dalada Maligawa* (Temple of the Tooth) to another. Devout Buddhists have never believed that the real Tooth was pulverized and burned as an idolatrous object by the Catholic Portuguese. One tradition is that the Relic was miraculously restored and transported back to Ceylon; another is that the Tooth captured in Jaffna was spurious. Tennent insists that the account of the capture and destruction of the Tooth is so well documented by the Portuguese annalists of the period that there can be no doubt that the Relic now deeply venerated in the Temple of the Tooth in Kandy is a substitute for the original.

In the seventeenth century the Portuguese, under constant attack by the nationalist Sinhalese, were faced with competition from another quarter. The Dutch, who looked with envious eyes on the prosperous trade of the Portuguese, which continued in spite of sieges and battles, arranged with the Kandyan kings to oust the hated Portuguese. The Dutch then built forts and harried the Portuguese on sea and land. In 1656, after the Dutch had kept Colombo under siege for almost seven months, nearly starving the garrison, the Portuguese finally surrendered.

The influence of the Portuguese in Ceylon was not a profound one. Except for the introduction of Catholicism, which continues to be the faith of more than six hundred thousand of Ceylon's native Christians (census of 1953), and family names like Fernando, Perera, and de Silva, common along the west coast of Ceylon, there is little today to show for the hundred and fifty years of predatory occupation. The Portuguese rule was marked by corruption, cruelty, and deplorable religious persecution. Yet the account is not altogether on the debit side. H. W. Codrington, in his *Short History of Ceylon,* says that the Catholic clergy were usually on the side of the people against their oppressors. "The fact that their converts, as in Japan, retained the Christian religion in spite of lack of clergy and active persecution by the Dutch," he declares, "speaks much in favor [of the Portuguese], and such a result cannot have come from a nation wholly bad." He gives the Portuguese credit for the introduction of chillies, tobacco, and foreign fruit trees, and expresses admiration for the courage of the small force of occupation which, in spite of the trying climate and the unrelenting hostility of the Sinhalese, succeeded in dominating so much of the island. It if had not been for the Portuguese, he believes, south India and Ceylon would almost certainly have fallen under Muslim rule.

The Dutch Occupation

The Dutch controlled Ceylon from 1656 to 1796. They were interested almost exclusively in trade. Having none of the Portuguese zeal for conversion to their way of life, they were fairly tolerant in their administration of those parts of the island that acknowledged their overlordship, though firm in their commercial transactions. They seized all the important coastal towns, built canals and forts, methodically took over the important cinnamon monopoly.

They ruled by military governors, representing the Dutch East India Company, whose main office was in Amsterdam. The Governor, who was responsible to the Company's Governor General in Java, divided Ceylon into three provinces with capitals in Galle, Colombo, and Jaffna. The Sinhalese system of local government by chiefs was retained, and a small civil service was trained to administer the various departments of government.

Like the Portuguese, the Dutch were harassed by the Kandyan Sinhalese, though the governors tried by flattery or force to come to peaceful terms with their unpredictable up-country neighbors. The Kandyans raided the coastal forts, and the Dutch retaliated, on one occasion capturing Kandy. Rajasinha II (1629–1687), the Sinhalese leader who gave the Dutch the most trouble, maintained a feudal court in Kandy.

Rajasinha was a brutal ruler, whose hatred for all white men was revealed in broken treaties, mistreatment of prisoners, cruel punishment of his own people who were friendly with the invaders. We know a great deal about him and the Sinhalese life of that day from the remarkable narrative written by a young Englishman, Robert Knox, who was held captive in Kandy for nearly twenty years between 1659 and 1679.

The Dutch, after futile efforts to appease the Kandyans, lost interest in the interior of the island and stayed close to the ports, from Matara in the south along the west coast to Jaffna in the north, from which Ceylon's still precious spices were shipped all over the world. They made no determined defense of the two major ports on the east coast, which were far from the cinnamon groves. The military interludes, for both the Portuguese and the Dutch, never interfered very much with trade.

During the eighteenth century the Dutch began to lose heart in their Ceylon enterprise, which was less profitable than the shareholders in the East India Company expected. In spite of their unhappy position, however, their homeland threatened by the wars in Europe that followed the French Revolution, hated by the defiant but weakened highland Sinhalese and by the subservient and hopeless lowland Sinhalese, they behaved like tidy businessmen and administrators. They set up a code of Roman-Dutch law, which is the basis of the legal system in Ceylon today. Having scant interest in the welfare of the people under their control, they provided only what government and public services were necessary. They established the Dutch Reformed Church in an effort to undermine the sturdy Catholicism which persisted after the Portuguese left and built a few schools which taught reading and writing and the Protestant catechism in Sinhalese. The teachers, both Dutch and indoctrinated Ceylonese, were more concerned with opposing Buddhism and Catholicism than with education.

In 1796 the Dutch Governor, J. G. van Angelbeek, either because of lack of spirit or because he had sold out, meekly surrendered to the British, who had been making hostile gestures towards the Dutch in Ceylon for some twenty years. Harry Williams, once a British planter in Ceylon, tartly sums up the Dutch occupation and their pusillanimous final defense:

> Whatever the details of the final collapse, it is certain that the Netherlands had had enough of Ceylon and were not, in the last analysis, prepared to die for it. They had put their faith in a common-sense trading policy and it had failed. Their end was far more inglorious than that of their predecessors, who died fighting to the very last. The truth is that they had not seen, in their search for wealth, that man does not live by bread alone.

The Dutch left almost as little behind them as the Portuguese. Their chief contributions were their system of law and the group known today as Burghers. The Dutch language, which its speakers tried to force upon the Ceylonese under their rule, is no longer spoken, even by the Burghers. On the other hand, Portuguese words survive, even among English speakers (e.g., "compound," from *campino,* the grounds attached to a house, and *almirah,* a wardrobe; other Portuguese words still in use by the Sinhalese are *kamisa,* shirt, *kalisan,* trousers, *mes,* stockings, *sapattu,* shoes). At the time of Tennent (mid-nineteenth century) what he called a corrupted Portuguese was still the vernacular of the middle classes in every coastal town of importance. Most of that speech has disappeared today. The Dutch, who had little real missionary spirit, made nominal Protestants of a few Sinhalese by giving certain offices only to men who professed their religion. This conversion was much less enduring than that of the Catholics, who still follow the faith and carry the names of their Portuguese baptismal sponsors. Ruins of Dutch forts may be seen today in places like Jaffna and Galle, and there are still a few Dutch houses and churches left. Among the treasures in some old homes are stout, brass-studded Dutch chests and secretaries. The physical evidence of nearly a century and a half of Dutch domination is meager indeed.

The British Period

The British had been in India for nearly two hundred years before they decided that a struggle with the Dutch over Ceylon was inevitable if the leadership of the British in the sub-continent was to be supreme. They came to Ceylon less interested in the spice trade than in possession of the superb harbor of Trincomalee, on the east coast, necessary to a great naval power giving military protection to its far-flung empire.

As early as 1763, with an eye on Trincomalee, they had tried to establish friendly relations with the Kandyan king. In 1782, Trincomalee, which was also coveted by the French, was captured by a British naval force, but returned to the Dutch two years later. In 1795 the Dutch listlessly prepared to move against the Kandyans, who had renewed hostilities. The Sinhalese king, Rajadhirajasinha (who like many of the later kings bore an Indian name), welcomed the opportunity to ally himself with the British. His objective was to drive out the Dutch, as his predecessor, the vigorous Rajasinha, one hundred fifty years earlier, had been helped by the Dutch to get rid of the Portuguese. The British took Trincomalee, then Jaffna, Negombo, and, in February, 1796, without a fight, Colombo itself.

At first the newly acquired territory was put under the direction of the British East India Company through a governor resident in Madras. Local government was carried out by British military governors, who brought with them Indians trained in the service of the East India Company. These Madrasi civil servants ignored the ancient traditional system of government through local chieftains which both the Portuguese and the Dutch had honored. The result was corruption, injustice, oppressive taxes, and humiliation at the hands of an enemy people hated and resisted for centuries before the Europeans appeared in Ceylon. This stupid policy was protested in a violent uprising of both highland and lowland Sinhalese, egged on by the French and the Dutch. The British, after attempting to put down the rebellion by bringing over Indian troops, finally realized that they had made a bad mistake, and in 1798 the Crown took over the administration of Ceylon from the East India Company, which, however, still continued to have a voice in the government.

The regime of the first civil governor, the Honorable Frederick North, was marred by a series of intrigues with unscrupulous Sinhalese pretenders to the throne, which resulted in murder, treachery, and general hatred of the British that lasted many years. There seems to be little doubt that the British during this period were guilty of grossly bad judgment.

The last of the Kings of Kandy, Sri Wickrama Rajasinha (1798–1815), a descendant of Tamil invaders, carried on a savage war with the British, which ended with his capture and deportation to India. With him the dynasty which had persisted in something less than a straight line for 2300 years came to an end.

One place in the old Kandyan kingdom is still a vivid reminder of the early days of British rule in Ceylon. It is a pierced rock on the road from Colombo to Kandy, as it winds upward into the rocky fastnesses which once guarded the all-but-impregnable Kandyan capital. Above it, overlooking the plains, is Scouts' Hill, from which the guardians of the passes into the mountains watched for the approach of hostile troops. The independent highland Sinhalese who had for centuries kept their well-protected boundaries from successful invasion—by Tamil warriors, by the Portuguese, by the Dutch, and, for almost twenty years, by the British—had an arrogant faith in their own security. Tennent says, "The power that crouched behind the mountains was regarded by the Europeans on the coast with a feeling of mystery and alarm; and mindful of the many calamities that had overtaken those who had made the attempt, the undertaking to scale them, should it ever become unavoidable, was regarded with gloomy apprehension." There was an ancient prophecy that anyone who should pierce the rock which blocked the pass into the mountains and make a road into Kandy from the plains would receive the kingdom as his reward. By 1825 the British had completed the road, blasting through the rock and fulfilling the prophecy. Every visitor to Ceylon today who goes by car from Colombo to Kandy must drive through the short tunnel which marked the end of the magnificent Kandyan kingdom.

Once they were in control of the entire island, the British began to make amends for their bad start by introducing a series of legal and political reforms that soon weakened the old feudal system. For the first time Ceylon was governed by a stable foreign power concerned with the health and well-being of its subjects, and not simply with conquest and exploitation. Instead of being tyrannically controlled by military governors appointed by the Portuguese authority in Goa or by the Dutch East Indian Company, Ceylon became a Crown Colony governed by a direct representative of the British sovereign. It was an integral part of the British Empire, a profitable colony, to be sure, but one whose human as well as natural resources were worth cultivating. A remarkable system of roads was built, forced labor was abolished, agriculture was fostered, schools were opened, and the excellent civil service which had been developed in India was opened to the Ceylonese. Into the wilderness of up-country Ceylon, as the coffee-industry prospered, railway lines were laid, a miracle of engineering.

G. C. Mendis says in his thoughtful little book, *Ceylon Today and Yesterday,* that the dividing line between the past and the present in Ceylon was drawn

in the Colebrooke Reforms of 1833, which put an end
to the feudal services owed to the king under the caste
system. No longer was a man bound to the land and
obliged to follow the occupation of his caste. A unified
government was established, doing away with the
three systems of administration that had existed previ-
ously, one in the Sinhalese Maritime Provinces, one
in the Tamil Maritime Provinces, one in the Kandyan
Provinces. A uniform system of courts replaced the
complex of legal authorities that had sprung up under
different rulers. The Governor, at first as autocratic
in the exercise of his power as his Dutch and Portuguese predecessors, and as the Sinhalese and Tamil
kings were from the very beginning, lost his judicial
powers and his control over monopolies which he had
inherited from the Sinhalese kings. With the establishment of Executive and Legislative Councils, he no
longer had absolute power over revenues and expenditures, and no longer did he make and administer the
laws. English was adopted as the official language and
established as the medium of instruction in some
schools. Some of the Sinhalese who learned English
became very important in the development of the new
colony as they learned the ideas of Western democracy
and began to apply them to their own country. Mendis,
dismissing the influence of the Portuguese and Dutch
as all but negligible (though he gives better marks to
the Dutch than to the Portuguese), says that the Cole-

brooke Reforms "led to radical changes in the economy of the country, in the system of civil or judicial administration, and in the structure of the Sinhalese and Tamil societies. They undermined the ancient Sinhalese and Tamil social systems and ushered in a new era of progress and prosperity."

First Steps Towards Self-Government

The Legislative Council set up under the Colebrooke Reforms was the first step towards a parliamentary government in Ceylon. The Council had no power, serving only as an advisory body. During the nineteenth century, there were frequent demands that the Council be given greater power, but little was done until the beginning of the present century. The increasingly larger and more influential Ceylonese middle class was dissatisfied with an administration in which all the high posts of the government were held by Europeans. In 1908, they asked for a reform of the Legislative Council, changing the representation from communal to territorial and making it elective rather than appointive. But the British were not yet ready to give even so reasonable and modest a part in the government to the Ceylonese, who, they thought, were too divided racially to govern themselves. The most they would concede at that time was a seat in the Council for an "Educated Sinhalese," who could speak, read, and write in English, and one additional seat each for Kandyan Sinhalese, Low-Country Sinhalese, and Tamils. Europeans, Burghers, and Educated Ceylonese were granted the franchise. Four members of the Legislative Council of 1912 were elected to office. The new Council was the first to have members with independent votes, but it was still mainly an advisory body.

Five years later the articulate, educated Ceylonese, now organized in their first democratic political party, the Ceylon National Congress, asked for a Legislative Council representing districts, in which the Ceylonese could have a majority. They also wanted elected Ceylonese members of the Executive Council. The British, however, were still unwilling to have the Governor's power in any way diminished. They granted what seemed to be representative government in 1921, but actually kept majority control through European and nominated membership in the Legislative Council. The Ceylon National Congress refused to cooperate with the Government on the grounds that the new system held no promise of even the beginnings of national self-government. Patriotic leaders, well acquainted with the evolution of Western democracy, had risen among the Ceylonese, both Sinhalese and Tamil. They opposed what they believed was oppression by the colonial government. As early as 1915 there had been communal riots, which the British thought were aroused by rebellion against their rule. They threw into prison the leaders, among them some of the most outspoken advocates of Ceylonese independence, including the two great Senanayake brothers, one of whom later became Ceylon's first Prime Minister; the Tamil leaders, Sir Ponnambalam Arunachalam and Sir Ponnambalam Ramanathan, also brothers, though not imprisoned, were "detained" by the British. Ruthless suppression of the demonstrations gave new spirit to the movement towards self-government. The feeling of the people during the four decades before Ceylon became in fact an independent nation has been well expressed by another Sinhalese patriot, Sir John Kotelawala, who was later to become Ceylon's third Prime Minister:

> No doubt the British planters, with the aid of Indian labour and of a Government that looked after the interest of foreign investors very well, had done a lot for the development of industries that increased the country's revenue. But was that a good reason for neglecting the basic needs of the permanent population, for resenting the claims and thwarting the aspirations of Ceylonese, and for insulting and humiliating them in their own country?

In 1924, Ceylon was granted the first Legislative Council in which more than half the members were elective. Elected members had to be British subjects over twenty-five, able to speak, read, and write English, with an annual income of not less than Rs. 1500 (about $300). The franchise was given only to male British subjects, not less than twenty-one years of age, able to read and write English, Sinhalese, or Tamil, with an annual income of not less than Rs. 600 (about $120). The new power was, of course, vested in the English-educated middle class.

When the Donoughmore Commission was appointed in 1927 to study the Constitution of 1924, which had not proved satisfactory, it discovered that only 4 percent of the population had the vote. Moreover, the Governor was still the supreme power through the Executive Council, consulting the Legislative Council as infrequently as possible. The Donoughmore Commission condemned the Constitution of 1924 as satisfactory neither to the Ceylonese nor to the British because it divorced power from responsibility.

The Donoughmore Constitution of 1931, which grew out of the report of Lord Donoughmore's Commission, granted the franchise to every man and woman over twenty-one, making Ceylon the first country in Asia to have universal suffrage. The State Council consisted of fifty elected and eight nominated members, divided into seven Executive Committees. The Chairmen of the Committees, together with three British Officers of State, formed the Board of Ministers. The Committee system was a departure from British parliamentary development and did not work well, as the old Legislative Council, which adopted the Donoughmore Constitution by a majority of only two, foresaw. The Tamils in Jaffna boycotted the elections of 1931 because they thought that the new Constitution did not go far enough in the direction of self-government. As Sir Ivor Jennings and H. W. Tambiah have pointed out in their book on the development of Ceylon's laws and constitution, "The Donoughmore Constitution had few friends at its beginning and none at all at the end. It had nevertheless some advantages. It covered the awkward gap between representative government and responsible government. It enabled the Ceylonese Ministers to take some of the steps—especially in the fields of education and health—which they thought were necessary. It gave them a broad experience of the problems of government. It taught them the necessity for co-ordination and common action."

In 1942, during the war, in which Ceylon's efforts on behalf of the Allies were invaluable, the State Council asked for dominion status. The Board of Ministers, under the guidance of D. S. Senanayake, drew up a draft Constitution which it declared was an acceptable compromise of the various points of view. In 1944, the British Government appointed a new Commission, under the direction of Lord Soulbury, to study the Ministers' draft and consult with the minority groups. The Soulbury Commission spent several months in Ceylon in 1944–5 and finally approved the Ministers' Constitution short of dominion status, making minor amendments and adding a weak Second Chamber to the State Council. The Constitution of 1947 provided for a Parliament consisting of the Governor, representing the King, a House of Representatives with 101 members, of whom ninety-five were elected and six appointed, and a Senate of fifteen members elected by the House and fifteen appointed by the Governor. The Executive Committee system was replaced by a cabinet form of government.

Independence

The Constitution of 1947 had been in operation for only a few months when the British Government, at Mr. Senanayake's repeated request, conferred Dominion ("fully responsible") status on Ceylon. In December, 1947, the Ceylon Independence Act was passed by the Parliament of the United Kingdom, and Ceylon became an independent nation on February 4, 1948. Her first Prime Minister was Don Stephen Senanayake, leader of the movement towards independence, deeply loved as the Father of the Nation, member of one of Ceylon's most distinguished Sinhalese families. The first Governor-General was Sir Henry Moore, who had been appointed Governor in 1944. He was succeeded by Lord Soulbury in 1949. Ceylon's first Ceylonese Governor-General, Sir Oliver Goonetilleke, came into office in 1954.

Mr. Senanayake had organized the United National Party, a coalition of several communal groups, in 1946, which he had led to victory after independence. He died in office in 1952 and was succeeded by his son, Dudley, who carried the UNP to a decisive victory in the elections of that year and then resigned in 1953 because of illness. Sir John Kotelawala, related by marriage to the Senanayake family, became Prime Minister and led the right-of-center, pro-West, pro-British government until the elections of 1956. In these the UNP was unexpectedly and overwhelmingly defeated, and a new government, dominated by the Mahajana Eksath Peramuna (MEP) or People's United Front, another coalition group, was formed under the leadership of S. W. R. D. Bandaranaike. The new Prime Minister had been a minister in Senanayake's first cabinet, but had broken with the UNP in 1951 to form the nationalistic, Buddhist, left-of-center Sri Lanka Freedom Party.

Since 1956 Ceylon has had increasing political and economic difficulties. Communal rivalry, which for hundreds of years had been quiescent, flared into violence. Some Sinhalese were resentful of what they felt was the disproportionate importance of Tamils in the civil service, the professions, and trade. Adoption of the "Sinhalese Only" Act of June, 1956, making Sinhalese the only official language, set off bloody riots, especially in recently colonized agricultural areas, where the predominantly Tamil population felt that they were being displaced by Sinhalese. A new and aggressive Tamil Federal Party, demanding a federal form of government and adoption of Tamil as an official language, threatened to call a nation-wide *satyagraha* ("civil disobedience"), a sit-down strike, supposedly non-violent, on a large scale. The Prime Minister came to uneasy terms with the Tamils in 1957, but during the summer of 1958 the communal tensions broke out again in savage clashes. After five days of unrestrained, hateful fighting between scattered groups of Sinhalese and Tamils, many of them gangs of thugs and looters interested in personal advantage, not in issues, the government declared a state of emergency and quickly restored order. The emergency continued into 1959.

The editor of *The Ceylon Observer,* Tarzie Vittachi, summed up the situation in Ceylon in September, 1958 in a short book, *Emergency '58.* Written in the heat of the conflict, before the causes—and results—were clear, it is overly emotional and alarmist, but dramatically reveals the gravity of the situation. Vittachi's pessimistic point of view is evident is such opinions as the following:

> Ceylon is now afflicted by a general malaise which no one can escape sensing. National unity has been shattered. The racial and religious tolerance which leavened our relationships has been sacrificed for political expediency. Increasing poverty and unemployment have brought the people to the brink of Communism. The next outbreak of violence may not be racial or even religious. During the latter days of the 1958 riots the attack was directed noticeably against Government officials and the middle class. The pattern is

clear. Unless the Government is able to open up new avenues for employment, increase the productivity of the island quickly and effectively, maintain law and order without succumbing to sectional and separatist demands, when violence breaks out again, it is likely that Ceylon's system of parliamentary democracy will be thrown away for something more "efficient" and ruthless.

These unhappy events, arousing passions that will be long in abating, involved other ethnic groups and, of course, seriously affected the national economy. The government of Prime Minister Bandaranaike was shaken by the civil disturbances, to which the terrible floods of 1957 added more misery and destruction of crops. *The New York Times* reported on January 1, 1958, that 650,000 acres of paddy had been flooded and 400,000 tons of rice destroyed, 75 percent of the year's crop. The floods left 700,000 people homeless. The government was also weakened by serious labor troubles. Nevertheless, it would not face new elections, unless forced into them by a crisis that the majority party could not handle, until 1961.

On September 25, 1959, however, a Buddhist priest shot and killed Prime Minister Bandaranaike a few days before he was to leave for the United States to address a meeting of the General Assembly of the United Nations and to hold conversations with President Eisenhower. The assassin's motivation was not immediately determined. The Governor General proclaimed a state of emergency and asked the Minister of Education, Wijayananda Dahanayake, to serve as Prime Minister. The new Prime Minister, a member of the Sri Lanka Freedom Party, had once been a Trotskyite Marxist, but had abandoned his associates to become an active anti-communist. He took over a government with a very slender majority in the Parliament because Bandaranaike's coalition government had lost its extreme leftist support several months before his death. The Dahanayake government was further weakened in the aftermath of Bandaranaike's murder, and on December 4, 1959 the Governor-General dissolved the Parliament. The national election held in March 1960 gave no party a clear majority, but the new government was again headed by Dudley Senenayake. Ceylon's trend leftward was halted.

4. Government and Politics

Ceylon is a self-governing member of the British Commonwealth. The government is officially carried on by the Queen, represented by the Governor-General, now a Ceylonese, who ostensibly has little power and does not participate except as an advisor in the actual administration of the country; * by a Parliament of two Houses, which has the authority to pass laws; and by a Cabinet which puts the laws into operation. The Governor-General is appointed by the Queen on the advice of the Prime Minister.

Ceylon's Parliamentary form of government is based on the United Kingdom and other Commonwealth

---

* During the disturbances of 1958, however, the Governor-General, Sir Oliver Goonetilleke, was given extraordinary powers by the Prime Minister to assist in controlling the critical situation.

models. Executive power is vested in the Cabinet, which is responsible to the popularly elected House of Representatives. The administration of government is carried out by a career civil service. The judiciary is independent of the executive and legislative branches. In accepting self-government, Ceylon did not withdraw as far as India and Pakistan did, continuing to recognize the Queen as sovereign as well as Head of the Commonwealth.

The Cabinet

The Cabinet is headed by the Prime Minister, who customarily also serves as Minister of Defense and External Affairs. He is appointed by the Governor-General as leader of the party which controls sufficient strength to form a government. The other ministers were thirteen in number in 1958, representing Finance; Justice; Home Affairs; Commerce and Trade; Local Government and Cultural Affairs; Posts, Broadcasting, and Information; Transport and Works; Education; Labor, Housing, and Social Services; Agriculture and Food; Lands and Land Development; Health; and Industries and Fisheries, Cabinet Ministers are members of Parliament selected by the Governor-General on the advice of the Prime Minister. The Prime Minister does not usually function as Leader of the House, as he does in the British Parliament. He appoints one Cabinet Minister to act as Leader of the

House and another as Leader of the Senate, under his guidance. Each of the Leaders is assisted by a party whip, whose job is to make certain that the government has a majority on all important issues.

Parliament

The Parliament, which is essentially the same as that recommended in 1947 by the Soulbury Commission, consists of a Senate and a House of Representatives. The Senate has thirty members, of whom fifteen are elected by the House of Representatives and fifteen appointed by the Governor-General. Senators serve for a period of six years, one-third retiring after every two years. Those appointed by the Governor-General, always on the advice of the Prime Minister, must be persons who "have rendered distinguished services" or are eminent "in professional, commercial, industrial, or agricultural life, including education, law, medicine, science, engineering, and banking." The House has 101 members, ninety-five popularly elected and six appointed by the Governor-General to insure representation of minority groups. All citizens of Ceylon over twenty-one are entitled to vote for members of the House in the present eighty-nine electoral districts (five constituencies have more than one member). In January, 1959, the House of Representatives passed a constitutional amendment bill, calling for the reorganization of parliamentary constituencies to increase the strength of the House from 101 to 150. At the end of 1959, however, the reorganization had not yet been put into effect. The provision for four additional Indian Tamil members after sufficient members of that community should qualify as citizens was abolished in 1959.

The duration of the House is five years unless Parliament is dissolved earlier. The Speaker of the House is elected for the duration of the Parliament from among the members, as are the Deputy Speaker, who is also the Chairman of Committees, and the Deputy Chairman of Committees. The Speaker presides over debates and may serve on certain committees. He may vote only in the event of a tie, and then only to keep the question open.

A money bill must be introduced in the House of Representatives, but any other bill may be introduced in either chamber. Normally, the House does not accept amendments made by the Senate, which actually has little power. Its function is mainly to delay too hastily conceived bills originating in the House. The delay is limited to one month for money bills and up to a year (until the next session of Parliament) for other types of legislation.

The Judiciary

The judicial system, like the executive and legislative branches of government, was patterned after the British model. The highest authority, in theory, is the Queen's Privy Council in England, but few cases are carried beyond the indigenous courts. These consist of a Supreme Court, Commissioners of Assize, a Court of Criminal Appeals, District Courts, and various subordinate courts. The Minister of Justice is responsible to Parliament for the administration of all the courts except the Supreme Court.

The Supreme Court consists of a Chief Justice and eight Puisne (Associate) Judges. It is a court of record and also has appellate and revisionary jurisdiction over civil cases, and both original and appellate jurisdiction over all criminal proceedings. All serious criminal offenses are tried by the Supreme Court itself. Whenever the Chief Justice so recommends, a Commissioner of Assize, with all the privileges and powers of Supreme Court Justices, may be appointed to preside over the criminal sessions of the Supreme Court for a specified period. These are held before one judge and a jury of seven persons. Appeals from the Assize Courts, as they are called, are heard by three or more judges of the Supreme Court sitting as a Court of Criminal Appeal.

The twenty-five District Courts can try all cases not exclusively reserved for the Supreme Court, particularly civil cases. In criminal cases, the limit of the District Courts' authority is punishment not exceeding two years' imprisonment, fines not exceeding Rs. 1000 (about $200), whipping, or a combination of these punishments.

Subordinate courts include thirty civil Courts of Requests; twenty-eight Magistrates' Courts trying minor criminal cases in which the punishment does not exceed fines of more than Rs. 200 ($40) or imprisonment not exceeding twelve months or whipping for those under sixteen; Rural Courts, which are outgrowths of old Sinhalese village tribunals; Muslim *Kathi* Courts, which have jurisdiction only in family and personal relations under Muslim law; and quasi-judicial bodies such as labor courts.

The criminal and civil codes are based on English law, retaining many elements of the Roman-Dutch civil law in effect when the British took over Ceylon from the Dutch. Matters of personal law, as under Dutch and colonial British rule, are settled under a system of Kandyan law for Kandyan Sinhalese, under Tamil law for Jaffna Tamils, and under Islamic law for Muslims. Low-country Sinhalese and the Tamils of the Eastern Province are subject to the common law of the country, which is Roman-Dutch as modified by English law.

The legal profession in Ceylon is divided into two branches, as in England: advocates and proctors. Advocates have functions like those of British barristers, who plead cases before courts; the proctors are like solicitors, who carry out legal duties other than that of pleading the cases.

Local Government

From the earliest period of Ceylon's history, village affairs were settled in open meetings of the leading senior citizens. The Village Councils, called *Gansabhas,* were not controlled by the king or by any other central authority. Only serious crimes were brought to the attention of the king. The *Gansabhas,* similar to New England town meetings, permitted matters of local interest to be fully discussed. Their decisions, determined by majority votes, were manifestations of the democratic instinct among the Ceylonese which brought about the present form of popular government.

Under the Portuguese and Dutch the Village Councils declined. The British, however, began to revive them about 1871, giving them more and more local authority. Today four types of local organizations exist: Village Committees in rural areas, Town Councils in rural towns, Urban Councils in urban towns, and Municipal Councils in highly developed urban areas. In 1957 all of Ceylon's more than 25,000 square miles except 192 were under Village Committee administration, bearing witness to the essentially rural character of the country. The Municipal Councils in the seven cities of Ceylon: Colombo, Kandy, Galle, Jaffna,

Kurunegala, Nuwara Eliya, and Negombo, are highly developed governing bodies concerned with the comfort and welfare of the people and with promotion of public health, public utility services, and public thoroughfares. They are virtually autonomous under the central government.

Parties and Politics

The first modern political parties in Ceylon developed during the late British period as the movement towards independence gained momentum. In 1946, looking towards the first parliamentary elections, three of these groups, based on communal interests, were combined under the leadership of D. S. Senanayake to form the United National Party, or UNP, as it was commonly called. The constituent groups were the Sinhalese Party or Sinhala Maha Sabha, the Ceylon Muslim League, and the Ceylon National Congress, which had strong Tamil influence. The UNP won only forty-two seats of ninety-five in the House, but with the help of the Tamil Congress, the Labor Party, and some Independent members was able to control the Parliament and set up a government. The UNP was the dominant party under three Prime Ministers until 1956, when it was defeated by a new coalition group, the Mahajana Eksath Peramuna (MEP) or People's United Front, under the leadership of S. W. R. D. Bandaranaike.

In any Ceylonese government the diverse political interests of the country must be taken into consideration. The Ceylonese are very fond of politics and gather into a variety of political organizations, none of which have much power alone, but which in combination may gain or threaten control of the Parliament. The number of such parties is almost as bewildering as in France during the Fourth Republic. In all these groups the personalities of the leaders are generally more important than party organization or programs.

The first Opposition to the UNP consisted of the Ceylon Indian Congress, some Independents, and three Marxist parties, only one of them a Leninist-Communist group, the others so-called Trotskyite parties. When these widely disparate groups could not agree on a leader, one was finally appointed in 1950 by the Governor-General: Dr. N. M. Perera, leader of the major Trotskyite group, the Lanka Sama Samaja Party (LSSP) or Ceylon Equality Party. After the 1952 election, Mr. Bandaranaike, who had been a Minister of Local Government in the first UNP Cabinet and had resigned from the UNP to become leader of the Sri Lanka Freedom Party, led the Opposition until the election of 1956. Then, having combined his Sri Lanka Freedom Party with the second Trotskyite group, which had splintered away from the more moderate LSSP to become the Viplavakari Lanka Sama Samaja Party (VLSSP) or Revolutionary Ceylon

Equality Party, the All-Ceylon Bhasa Peramuna or Language Front, and a number of Independents to form the People's United Front, Mr. Bandaranaike and his allies decisively defeated the UNP and were invited to form the new government. The Opposition in the Parliament of 1956 consisted of the few members of the UNP who were re-elected, the LSSP members, led by Dr. Perera, who once more became the Leader of the Opposition, the Communists, and representatives of several Tamil groups.

This is not the place to analyze the political beliefs of the many parties which actively participate in Ceylon's elections. They differ on too many local issues to be easily understood by foreign observers. Some of the attitudes towards basic national and international policies, however, may help to explain some of Ceylon's recent crises. The UNP and other conservative groups continue to be strongly anti-communist. The UNP's chief spokesman after the death of D. S. Senanayake was Sir John Kotelawala, whose vigorous stand against the imperialist designs of communism on the free countries of Asia was one of the highlights of the Bandung Conference of Asian-African Nations in April, 1955. D. S. Senanayake, founder of the UNP, had demonstrated his government's fear of communist domination when he presided over the Commonwealth Foreign Ministers' meeting in 1950, which set up the Colombo Plan to raise "the living standards of Asia's peoples as the bulwark against the menace of Communism," as Sir John describes the meeting.

The UNP official line is that it wants Ceylon to be part of the Free World as a parliamentary democracy which guarantees political freedom. It believes in encouraging foreign investment as a means of developing the country's economy at the same time that the government itself launches major power, mining, and other projects. It accepts the idea of a welfare state in which social services are provided as far as the national finances can afford them. Under a UNP government, trade relations which had far-reaching consequences were set up with Communist China, but though friendly to all countries, including Russia and China, Ceylon sought no closer relationships than trade agreements. UNP Cabinets were predominantly Sinhalese, Buddhist, and Goyigama, the Kandyan Sinhalese conspicuous among them, with slight representation by Tamils and Muslims.

The MEP follows a nationalist-neutralist policy. It would like to make Ceylon a republic, acknowledging Queen Elizabeth as head of the Commonwealth, but not as sovereign. It is distinctly left of center and has strong support among the Buddhist, Sinhalese-speaking groups. The MEP goes along with some of the UNP ideas, but is alarmed by the entry of foreign capital, being more interested in eventually nationalizing present industries than in starting new ones with the help of foreign investors. It wants to hasten the establishment of Sinhalese as the sole official language. It has entered into diplomatic relations with the USSR and the People's Republic of China.

The various Tamil parties are deeply concerned with the subordination of their language and their position in Ceylonese society. The Tamil Federal Party, which won ten seats in the election of 1956, wants to set up a Tamil state in Ceylon which would be federated with the Sinhalese state. They protest against the Sinhalese domination of the Tamils under the present constitution.

The various leftist parties, though they differ radically among themselves about the means of reaching their objectives, have the standard Marxist faith in equitable distribution of wealth, in socialization of natural resources and private industry, in the establishment of a communist republic. The Communist Party, of course, follows the Moscow line. The VLSSP seems to be moving closer to the Communist Party, compromising its associates in the MEP. The LSSP wants to set up a government of workers and peasants that would not be dominated by any foreign government. It is strictly a nationalist, proletarian party, which believes in a sort of Marxian idealism quite different from the tenets of Sino-Soviet communism. All three leftist parties use the symbol of the hammer and sickle, even though they are far from presenting a united front.

In 1952 the UNP won fifty-four seats in the House, which with the support of sympathetic members of other parties gave it a tremendous majority. During the next four years, growing complacent with what seemed to be an invincible position of public approval, the UNP lost some of its support by reducing the subsidy on rice and doing away with free lunches in the schools. It became identified with the rich and privileged and less and less with the common people. Under heavy criticism, it nevertheless faced the election of 1956 with confidence. Its severe defeat, losing all but eight of its seats in the House, came as a surprise not only to the Party leadership but to the foreign diplomatic corps, which had closely watched political developments. As a result of the election the distribution of seats in the new Parliament was as follows:

Mahajana Eksath Peramuna	51
Lanka Sama Samaja Party	14
Tamil Federal Party	10
United National Party	8
Independents	7
Communist Party	3
Tamil Congress Party	1
Tamil Resistance Front	1

Critical Political Problems

Ceylon is a very young country, taking her place in the complex pattern of twentieth century international stresses. The people of this new nation have not yet decided just where they fit into the pattern. They are undergoing severe political growing pains. The party system has not yet acquired the stability and maturity it will need to cope successfully with the dismaying problems of economic development, the world-wide threat to the democratic principles for which the Ceylonese have always stood, the responsibility of enlightened leadership in Asia and her awakening sister-continent, Africa, the delicate relationship between India and Ceylon, and a multitude of vexing domestic issues.

Thus far in her national youth Ceylon has produced a heterogeneous collection of political groups, some of them frankly concerned only with local special interests, others mixing idealism with cynicism, radical thinking with reactionary thinking, socialism and communism with capitalism. The extraordinary nature of Ceylon's politics is well illustrated in the fact that the most vital party outside of the coalition groups that have formed all governments since 1948 is Dr. Perera's moderate Trotskyite Marxist party which rejects international communism even more vehemently than it rejects capitalism. This group has splintered several times as firebrands demanded more revolutionary doctrines and formed new parties or joined more radical old ones. Nevertheless, the LSSP has managed to keep its integrity, steadfastly professing a nationalist radical socialism without surrender to the pressures of international communism. Dr. Perera, a Buddhist and sincere patriot, who has been a successful mayor of Colombo, is one of Ceylon's most respected leaders.

The greatest danger to Ceylon as it works out its destiny is that it may be warped out of its own natural course by foreign influences that will take advantage of the leaders' inexperience and the innocent, sometimes indolent trustfulness of the Ceylonese people.

Ceylon's government must take into consideration several major international involvements at the same time that it faces critical domestic difficulties:

The Ceylon-India dispute over citizenship for Indian Tamils. No satisfactory solution to this cause of conflict with India has been found. A pact signed in 1954 required that India check illegal entry of impoverished Indian laborers into relatively prosperous Ceylon and that Ceylon liberalize her citizenship laws, accepting at least the grandchildren of immigrants born in Ceylon as citizens. The large number of those not recognized as citizens of either country is a source of continuing friction.

United Nations membership. Barred from membership in the U. N. by Soviet vetoes until December,

1955, Ceylon has been an active member since that time, taking enthusiastic interest in technical assistance programs, disarmament, intercultural relations, etc. Her delegate to the United Nations until 1958, Ambassador R. S. S. Gunawardene, was a member of the committee which wrote the memorable report on Soviet aggression in Hungary in 1957.

"Friendly relations with all nations, but non-involvement with any power bloc." This official government position requires a delicate sense of balance that becomes more difficult to maintain as the world situation shifts. Some of the international communist front groups that have picked Ceylon as their headquarters or as the site of major meeting, such as the Afro-Asian Writers' Bureau, the World Federation of Democratic Youth, and the International Association of Democratic Lawyers, are a source of embarrassment to a strictly neutral government.

Colombo Plan membership. In Ceylon, where the Plan originated in 1950, the seventeen-nation organization maintains its Council for Technical Cooperation in South and Southeast Asia, its Bureau for Technical Cooperation, and its Information Unit.

British Commonwealth status as a member nation of the Commonwealth or as a republic. Ceylon's tie with the U. K. is still very strong.

Relationship with the Sino-Soviet bloc. The Rubber-Rice Trade Agreement with China in 1952 has resulted in marked changes in Ceylon's traditional pattern of trade. The diplomatic and economic influence of China and the U.S.S.R. is growing.

Relationship with the United States. The cordial diplomatic, economic, and cultural relations between Ceylon and the United States will doubtless continue as an important factor in Ceylon's foreign policy.

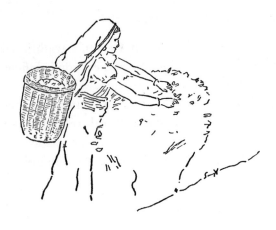

5. *The National Economy*

The economy of Ceylon depends largely upon three agricultural export commodities, two of which have developed significantly only within the past hundred years: tea, rubber, and coconut. The income derived from these exports is necessary to buy food, which Ceylon does not produce in sufficient quantities to feed herself. More than half the rice needed in the national diet, which depends on large amounts of rice, must be imported from Burma and China. The land which might be used to increase production of rice and other food-crops has been increasingly diverted to the money-crops, until two-thirds of all cultivated land and two-thirds of the entire population are occupied by production, associated industry, and distribution of the three crops. In a flourishing world market the failure of the country to grow sufficient food would be unimportant since the profit on relatively valuable exports would comfortably pay for low-cost imports. Tea, however, now covers most of the available hill-slopes suitable for its cultivation; natural rubber is an uncertain commodity because of the advance of synthetics; and past neglect of conservation—new planting and elimination of old, tired trees—has cut down production of both rubber and coconuts.

Meanwhile the population is increasing at a furious rate, from eight million in 1953 to an estimated thirteen and one-half million in 1972. Between 1946 and 1958, almost three million new mouths had to be fed, with only small increase in the acreage devoted to production of food.

The threat to the nation's standard of living is not yet critical. There is still room for expansion as the Dry Zone once again becomes fertile under completed irrigation projects, some new, some the restored tanks of the early Sinhalese kings. The crowded southwest quarter of the island will have to spill over into less attractive areas, where work will be harder and yields less than in the lushly green and prosperous areas, well watered by the rains of the southwest monsoon. Already, however, the warnings of unemployment and hunger have been heard and heeded by the government, which is desperately looking for ways to increase and diversify production before the trouble which began in 1958 over communal rivalry is intensified by the threat of famine.

Only about four in ten Ceylonese are gainfully occupied. The remaining six are too young, too old, ill, or unemployed. Those gainfully employed are distributed roughly as follows: agriculture, 50 percent; hunting, fishing, forestry, 3 percent; industry and mining, 11 percent; trade, transport, banking, 21 percent; service occupations: civil service, medicine, education, police, military and domestic service, 15 percent.

Agriculture

Of the island's total area of 16,250,000 acres, about 3,700,000 acres are under cultivation, and three million more acres might be developed with improved methods and increased supply of water. If the present ratio of tea, rubber, and coconut land to land devoted to food production continues, only a million additional acres will be planted in edible crops, not nearly enough to take care of the population increase. At present, 60 percent of the farmers produce export crops such as the Big Three, plus tobacco, cinnamon, and citronella. Twenty percent grow rice, producing twenty-eight million bushels in 1956, less than half of the island's consumption. The average yield per acre for two crops a year was only 31.14 bushels in 1956, which could be greatly increased by intensive cultivation, improved methods, better fertilization, etc. A very small number of farmers grow vegetables as their main crop or raise cattle and buffaloes. There are some marginal, catch-as-catch-can farmers who grow a little rice, keep some chickens, wait for a few coconuts to ripen. Some depend on wasteful *chena* farming, clearing sections of jungle land by burning, leaving in the stumps. After a few meagre crops, mostly cereals like *kurakkan* and maize, the land is abandoned, and the cultivator tries again somewhere else.

Small-scale cultivation produces most of the rice, fruit, vegetables, and other foodstuffs, as well as a considerable amount of the rubber, coconut, and the less important cash-crops. This type of cultivation accounts for about 55 percent of all agricultural workers. The rest are employed on estates, usually those growing tea and rubber.

In 1952, at the request of the Ceylon government, the International Bank for Reconstruction and Development sent a mission to Ceylon under the direction of Sir Sydney Caine. The five hundred-page report of this mission, *The Economic Development of Ceylon,* published in 1953, is the most comprehensive study of Ceylon's economy ever made. Some of the findings of that Mission which still apply will be referred to in this chapter.

Tea

Tea is the most important of Ceylon's products, amounting to about two-thirds of the country's exports. Ceylon is the second largest producer of tea in the world, growing more than 30 percent of the world's tea. Only India produces more. In 1956, tea production amounted to over 376 million pounds, of which 26 million pounds were consumed at home. Of the three and one-half million acres under cultivation, about 565,000 are devoted to tea (660,000 to rubber, one million to coconuts). Most of the tea is grown on estates of a hundred acres or more, employing about 500,000 laborers, most of them Tamils from India.

Tea has been grown on a large scale in Ceylon only since about 1880. After the decline of the spice trade, an important crop was coffee, which grew wild. Both the Portuguese and the Dutch exported small quantities of coffee. The British greatly expanded the coffee industry, and by 1877 over a quarter of a million acres of coffee were planted, yielding a million pounds a year of high-quality coffee. In that year appeared a fungus blight which destroyed the leaves of the plant and within ten years laid waste the estates that had been developed at great cost in labor and money. Within five years coffee land was switched over to the growing of tea, and by the end of the century 384,000 acres were planted in tea. This dramatic change, which made use of the fine roads and estate organization established by the British, is a great tribute to the courage, initiative, and resourcefulness of the pioneer planters who turned a catastrophe into a tremendously profitable new industry, the prime source of modern Ceylon's prosperity.

Low-country tea grows up to 1500 feet above sea-level; it is an abundant crop but of medium quality. Mid-country tea grows up to 3500 feet. High-grown tea, on slopes from 3500 to 7000 feet, is the least productive but generally the best in quality. The tea, made from the dark green, glossy, young leaves and buds of carefully kept bushes, is processed in up-country factories by withering, rolling, fermenting, and firing. All Ceylon tea is black, sorted into the various grades of Broken Orange Pekoe, Orange Pekoe, Pekoe, Souchong, Fannings, and Dust. Most of it is blended, the high-grown, delicate teas being mixed with the fuller-bodied teas grown on the lower slopes.

Up to the time of Independence most tea estates were owned by British planters or by corporations which employed experienced British overseers. Big estates are like miniature kingdoms, having their own dispensaries, maternity hospitals, schools, crèches or day nurseries for the children of working women, temples, bakeries, shops. The superintendents, or "Big Masters," and their assistants, "Little Masters," live well in fine houses, often with breath-taking views of the mountain scenery, waited on by many servants, dining in style, gathering occasionally for cricket or tennis or golf and a few drinks at nicely appointed clubs. They have considerable power over the workers. An estate of 1400 acres has an average of 3200 bushes to the acre, requiring the labor of about 1500 men, women, and children to cultivate, prune, manure, terrace, and pluck the tea, to work in the factory, and to perform community services.

Since Independence European ownership has decreased as the new government began a process of "Ceylonizing" the estates, requiring more and more trained Ceylonese as "creepers" (apprentices), prior to becoming "Little Masters," some of whom have become "Big Masters." In 1956 ownership of the acreage was divided as follows: foreign companies, 30 percent; joint Ceylonese and European companies, 15 percent; non-Ceylonese individuals, 16 percent; individual Ceylonese, 27 percent; holdings under ten acres owned by individual Ceylonese, 12 percent.

The International Bank Mission of 1952 reported that for Ceylon to keep its tea production at its past profitable high level, costs must be reduced rather than acreage increased. It also recommended that the tendency towards fragmentation of estates, caused by prevailing inheritance laws and customs, which has occurred as tea estates are transferred from European to Ceylonese owners, should be halted by a clear government policy. It emphasized the continuing importance of research on and application of soil conservation methods, fertilizing, and pruning.

Rubber

After tea, rubber is second in importance, amounting to 17.7 percent of the country's exports. Ceylon was the birthplace of the rubber industry in the East. The first rubber was grown in 1876 from seeds imported from South America, planted in England, and taken to Ceylon as young plants. Some of the original trees still stand in the Henaratgoda Botanical Gardens, at Gampaha, not far from Colombo. Those trees were the ancestors of all the rubber trees of the Far East. Malaya, Indonesia, and Thailand have become far more important exporters of rubber than Ceylon, which produces only about 5 percent of the world's natural rubber. During World War II, however, with all other Asian rubber under Japanese control, Ceylon was an important supplier of rubber for the Allied Nations.

About 660,000 acres of Wet Zone land along the southwest coast and up to 2000 feet of the hill slopes are planted in rubber, which requires a hot, moist climate. More than 65 percent of the acreage planted in rubber is owned by Ceylonese planters; most of the rest is owned by Europeans. In 1936 the figures were reversed.

Rubber trees, which grow to a height of a hundred

feet, are planted in dark, damp groves. Early in the morning they are tapped, usually by Tamil men and women, who make deft diagonal incisions in the bark so that the milky latex flows downwards towards a half-coconut shell. Working quickly, because the latex ceases to flow after mid-morning, and with great attention to cleanliness, the laborers collect the latex in pails and take it to the factory for processing into smoked sheet or crepe rubber.

The International Bank Mission of 1952, noting that natural rubber is of diminishing value in world trade, recommended improved methods of production, increased research, improvement of estates by new planting and elimination of old, low-producing trees under the Rubber Rehabilitation Scheme, which has been in operation since 1950. An extensive program of rubber development was begun in 1957 with the help of a loan from the People's Republic of China.

A major part of Ceylon's rubber since 1952 has gone to Communist China in return for rice. The trade agreement with China, which supplied a strategic material to a nation labeled aggressor by the United Nations (though at the time Ceylon was not a member of the U. N.), was prompted at the outset by economic necessity. Sir John Kotelawala has explained that the drop in the world market of the price of natural rubber seriously threatened Ceylon's national income. At the same time she had to buy rice in a rising market.

China needed rubber, for which she was willing to pay a high price, exchanging it for rice at a price lower than that demanded by Burma, Ceylon's traditional supplier. Sir John has declared that the alternative to this deal, which for a time inhibited American economic aid to Ceylon, would have been "just plain starvation." In 1957, 10 percent of Ceylon's total exports, almost entirely rubber, went to the People's Republic of China. Between 1952 and 1957, Ceylon annually sent 50,000 tons of sheet rubber to China, receiving in exchange 270,000 metric tons of rice. Under a new five-year agreement, signed in 1957, China provides 200,000 tons of rice in exchange for 20,000 tons of rubber each year.

Coconuts

Ceylon's third most important money crop is the only one of the three native to Ceylon, which serves the people and is also abundant enough for extensive export, and which is owned and processed by Ceylonese rather than by foreigners. Unlike tea and rubber, the nut-bearing palm trees have always grown in Ceylon, producing food, drink, rope, mats, fences, roofing, firewood, oil for light and for cooking, and beauty for even a poor man's yard. Domestic consumption of tea is only about 4 percent of the total production, of rubber only about 325 tons a year out of over 90,000. But the coconut is there for everybody to enjoy and to

145

use lavishly, and there is plenty left over to share with the rest of the world. Every person in Ceylon consumes about 140 coconuts a year, accounting for about 40 percent of the production. The rest are exported.

Coconut palms take up more than a million acres of the best island soil, mainly in the Wet Zone along the coast and up to 1500 feet above sea level. There is a saying in Ceylon that palm trees prefer to live within sight of the sea and close to the homes of people. Nowhere in the island do they grow so well as in the crowded southwest quarter, shading the village compounds and leaning their graceful trunks towards the sea. The cultivation of coconut groves is not a demanding occupation. The trees bear every two months, requiring relatively little care. Williams says that "there is less work done in the running of a coconut estate than in any other comparable enterprise in the world." As an up-country tea planter, used to the hardworking Tamil laborers on his estate, however, he was inclined to be scornful of the Sinhalese who, he says, prefer to raise coconuts, "the laziest way of earning a living to be found anywhere in this bustling world."

More than 80 percent of the land devoted to coconuts is in the hands of those who own less than twenty acres, many of them with only one or two precious trees. From those trees come over a hundred different products: the scraped meat of the nut is used everywhere in curries; the "cabbage" or unexpanded leaves make pickles and preserves; the immature nut produces medicine and candy, the mature nut a sweet "milk" that can be drunk and flesh that may be cooked. The sap of the tree becomes toddy and, when distilled, arrack. When the nuts are pressed, they provide oil for soap, lamps, and candles, and the mast from which the oil is extracted is fed to livestock. The shell itself makes charcoal, knife-handles, receptacles for latex, and the fiber around the shell becomes coir which makes rope, fishermen's nets, brushes, mats, etc. The leaves braided together make *cadjan,* used in fences and roofs, brooms, baskets, and so on. Finally, the wood is used for fuel and for doors, shelves, and other wooden parts of the houses. These are some of the domestic uses of this wonderful tree. For export are copra, made from the dried meat of the coconut, coconut oil, and desiccated coconut, the familiar shredded coconut sold around the world (but never tasting as good as when it is freshly prepared and sprinkled on a Ceylon curry).

Ceylon's production of coconuts is surpassed only by that of the Philippines, Indonesia, and India. Ceylon is the world's largest exporter of coir fiber and ranks third, after the Philippines and Indonesia, in exports of copra and coconut oil.

The International Bank Mission reported that the coconut industry in Ceylon is in drastic need of rehabilitation if it is not to decline. It recommended an intensive survey and classification of all coconut plantations, a program of replacement by new planting of up to 30,000 acres a year, and education of smallholders in proper methods of conservation, cultivation, and harvesting. Some of these recommendations are now being carried out, under government supervision.

Other Commercial Crops

Cacao, cinnamon, arecanut (used in the preparation of betel for chewing), citronella, pepper, nutmeg, papain (an enzyme used in medicines and meat tenderizers, from the papaya fruit), cardamons, cloves, tobacco, hemp, tumeric, ginger, chillies, *gingelly* (sesame), kapok, and cashew nuts account for only 5 percent of the total export of Ceylon. A little cotton is grown for domestic use, as are some vegetables, maize, sorghum, and millet. Sugar, except for a coarse grade made from the palm and a very small amount of sugar cane, wheat flour, and over half the rice must be imported. Some 90 percent of the peas, beans, lentils, curry-stuffs, and dried fish, which are important parts of most Ceylonese meals must also be imported.

Industry

There is little industry in Ceylon today, though the government is making some effort to encourage it. Not more than about 5 percent of the gross national product comes from manufacturing, which, exclusive of cottage industries, employs fewer than 60,000 workers. Under the government-sponsored Corporation Act of 1955, seven factories were set up to manufacture ceramic ware; vegetable oils; D.D.T., caustic soda, and chlorine; paper; leather goods; plywood, and cement. These factories were made autonomous at the end of 1956, and the government turned its attention to such projects as the establishment of a refinery for the separation of constituents of mineral sands such as ilmenite and monazite, a cotton-spinning mill, and a sugar refinery, and expansion of the cement industry, which now supplies only 80,000 tons of the needed 240,000 tons a year, and of the salt industry, which is a government monopoly.

The Department of Industries, concerned with the lack of opportunity outside of government for the employment of young educated men, has considered several types of manufacturing in partnership with private capital, both local and foreign. Among these are plants for the manufacture of confectionery, electric bulbs, dry-cell and wet-cell batteries, and bicycles. Private industry, with the help of foreign skill and capital, plans to manufacture razor blades, paper clips, pins, tubular furniture, and brown sugar. It is already active on a small scale in the production of tiles, aluminum ware, machine parts, leather, clothing, soap, rubber shoes, matches, paints, and cigars.

In addition to these small plants, which are largely experimental, part of the government's effort to diversify the island's occupations and to meet the challenge of an industrial age, there is a considerable amount of cottage industry, producing such things as pottery, textiles, baskets, toys, and rope. Nine private distilleries and one state-owned distillery produce over 800,000 gallons of arrack a year. This industry, like salt production, is a government monopoly, which brings in more excise revenue than any other commodity.

In order to stimulate industrial development which will help to protect Ceylon in the future even if there is a decline in the demand for her three principal commodities, the government established the Ceylon Development Finance Corporation in 1955, originally proposed by the International Bank Mission. The Finance Corporation, financed in part by sale of stock, partly by an International Bank loan, aids in the establishment of agricultural and industrial enterprises.

Also on the advice of the Bank Mission, a government-supported Scientific and Industrial Research Institute was set up to do essential research for both government agencies and private organizations. The Institute makes practical field and laboratory studies of local raw materials and their utilization, tests products, seeks by-products, cuts production costs and losses, gives technical advice to government departments and private enterprises, studies agricultural problems, and develops ideas for new industries. During 1957, it maintained four laboratories and had under way or completed thirty-four major long-term industrial research projects, eighteen governmental, the rest private. It also studied the feasibility of such agricultural projects as improved desiccation of coconut, rubber compounding and testing, production of sugar from sweet toddy, new sources of commercial vegetable oils, and improved distillation of citronella and cinnamon oil.

Supervision of these bodies and coordination of industrial and agricultural planning are under an Economic Committee of the Cabinet, assisted by an economic planning secretariat.

Mining

Ceylon is the world's leading producer of high-grade graphite. The Ceylon *Yearbook* claims that the island's graphite deposits are the biggest and most productive in the world and that for a time Ceylon was the world's principal source of this mineral. In 1956, however, there were only thirty-four graphite mines in operation, down from 452 mines in 1942, when nearly 28,000 tons were exported for war use, compared with 9,207 tons in 1956.

The most famous minerals of Ceylon are her gems, which have been important in the country's trade for many centuries. The mining of gems, however, is a highly speculative operation, carried out in a more or less unsystematic way in a small area around Ratnapura. But known of the gems are the sapphires and rubies, especially those in which certain structural irregularities produce six-pointed stars. Others are the chrysoberyls, including cat's-eyes and alexandrites; aquamarines; and the semi-precious stones, topaz, spinel, garnet, zircon, tourmaline, and moonstone.

Visitors to Ceylon who see only Colombo and Kandy are struck by the number of jewelers' shops which they see everywhere. They would do well to patronize only those which guarantee their stones and to realize that reputable gem dealers are well aware of the value of their wares and are not likely to offer the fantastic bargains tourists seem to expect. Let the buyer beware of plausible itinerant vendors who may appear almost anywhere, offering neatly wrapped jewels for low prices. Nevertheless, a perfect cornflower-blue sapphire or a set of matched aquamarines is the pure distillation of Ceylon's beauty, and those who can afford them, if the stones are genuine, would be foolish to resist. More cautious—and less affluent—visitors should be satisfied with inexpensive moonstones, antique pins set with pale rubies, or the coarser and less desirable smoky topazes.

Ceylon's mineral resources, though limited, will repay development. During the past few years potentially valuable deposits of ilmenite, monazite, and zircon have been found, though only monazite has been marketed. The high-grade iron ore in the southwestern part of the island has not yet been exploited. Large quantities of kaolin or china-clay are present in various areas. Geologists have discovered traces of several rare minerals, important in modern scientific research, particularly thorianite.

Tourism

The earnings from tourism during 1952 and 1953 made it Ceylon's fourth most important "export." The number of visitors to Ceylon in 1952 (482,000, including 416,236 transit passengers) has decreased since that time because of critical conditions in the Near East and because of the disturbances in Ceylon itself. As tensions are relaxed, however, and as the government becomes more experienced in attracting visitors, tourism should be an increasingly more important source of income. Ceylon is visited by many ships, and several airlines include it in their itineraries. Outside of Colombo, Kandy, and Nuwara Eliya, however, there are no first-class hotels. Travelers to other parts of the island, including the ruined cities, must be prepared for the quaintness, local color, and occasional primitive facilities of rest houses (a few are fairly well appointed and modern), maintained by the government.

Power

The Department of Government Electrical Undertakings operates three state power plants and supervises the development of private and municipal plants. The state plant at Laksapana is a hydroelectric project, which, when complete, will generate 150,000 kilowatts. It is financed by a loan from the International Bank for Reconstruction and Development. Another hydroelectric project is at Gal-Oya.

The hydroelectric power potential of Ceylon is not large, though the current 6 percent of total power from hydroelectric sources can be greatly expanded. The remainder of the power is supplied by steam plants, necessary because of the irregular rainfall and uncertain water flow in the rivers.

Transportation

Serving Ceylon are several international airlines under the flags of the United States, the United Kingdom, India, Australia, and the Netherlands, in addition to Ceylon's own international line, which operates in partnership with K.L.M. Royal Dutch Airlines. Three airports accommodate international flights, of which the busiest is that at Ratmalana, eight miles south of Colombo. Internal air service is maintained only between Colombo and Jaffna.

In 1956, the Port of Colombo ranked as the seventh busiest port in the British Commonwealth. The artificial harbor, one of the biggest in the world, had no quays for alongside berthing, modern warehouses, mechanical cargo-handling equipment, and other apparatus of a modern port until 1954, when the port facilities began to be modernized. In 1956 nearly 3000 ships from all over the world entered the Port of Colombo.

The Public Works Department maintains over 11,000 miles of the 14,000 miles of motorable roads in Ceylon, of which about half are bitumen surfaced. The number of motor vehicles in the country increased from less than 40,000 in 1947 to over 100,000 in 1957.

Much of the everyday travel in Ceylon is by bus. Regular service is offered over approximately one thousand routes. Visitors to Ceylon, however, are not advised to try this means of transportation unless they have a real taste for adventure. Bus travel is rather unpredictable so far as schedules are concerned, not very comfortable, and very crowded. One of the novel sights of Ceylon, interesting to the photographer or the student of folkways, but not to a traveler in need of transportation, is a special bus, decorated with sprays of precious coconut or arecanut buds, on its way to one of the many pilgrimage centers in festival time, full of happy, perspiring people.

Dating back to Portuguese and Dutch occupation are the canals of the west coast, which connect a series of small lakes, forming an inland waterway of about 120 miles.

The state-owned and controlled railroads of Ceylon are among the most interesting in the world, especially

155

the 150 miles of up-country lines. Automobile travel is undoubtedly the most pleasant and satisfactory way of seeing Ceylon, but the railroads are good, and the ride from Colombo to Peradeniya and from there through the spectacular highlands to the end of the line at Badulla is superb. No one could ever forget that trip, over deep gorges, through many tunnels, along the ridge at Haputale from which the sea may be seen far away on one side and the magnificent Uva Valley on the other, through tea plantations, into jungle, past skillfully terraced paddy fields.

In 1865, only forty years after the first railroad was opened in England, the British laid the first tracks in Ceylon. At that time there were fewer than one thousand miles of roads in the entire country. Neither the Dutch nor the Portuguese, who were interested only in the coastal region, had built many roads. Until the British began an intensive program of road-building early in the nineteenth century, there was no means of travel over long distances except by palanquins carried by elephants or coolie bearers. The first road to Kandy, we may recall, was put through by the British in 1825. The planters of coffee and, later, of tea were chiefly responsible for the construction of railroads. Before they came, the only way of transporting their crops to Colombo for shipment was by slow bullock cart. The task of laying embankments over paddy fields, bridging glens and gorges, cutting through rocks, and building tunnels over the seventy-four miles from Colombo to Kandy between 1858 and 1867 was heart-breaking in those early days of railroading.

The remainder of the 180 miles from Colombo to Badulla was built in sections, not being completed until 1924, going over very rough terrain up to a maximum height above sea level of 6,200 feet. G. F. Perera in 1925 wrote a romantic account of the coming of the railroad to Ceylon, unfortunately now out of print. His description of the up-country railroad journey might be used today in Tourist Bureau literature to tempt visitors:

> For a combination of tropical upland, mountain and low-land, pastoral and wooded scenery—for a succession of deep gorges and high mountain peaks, with streams dashing along cataract, waterfall, or quiet pool-like stretches—there are few railway rides in the world to compare with the Uva line.

About 750 miles of line serve the low country, all on broad gauge tracks except for an eighty-six mile stretch of narrow gauge. Over all lines travel twenty million passengers a year, most of them in crowded third-class compartments, on wooden benches, while the comfortable first-class compartments carry only a small part of the traffic.

Communications

All internal and external communications facilities are owned and operated by the government. More than half of the telephone subscribers in the island are in the Colombo area (similarly, nearly half the licensed motor vehicles are registered in and around Colombo), indicating that the remainder of the country is still very provincial. Telephone and cable connections with foreign countries, including the United States, are good.

The government also runs the broadcasting system, with headquarters in Colombo. Programs are broadcast over both a National Service, which follows the plan of the British Broadcasting Corporation, and an international Commercial Service, which is a source of important revenue through its advertising. The National Service has a School Broadcasting Service, which sends out educational programs in Sinhalese, Tamil, and English. Under an agreement with the United States Government, signed in 1951, in return for broadcasting equipment, including three thirty-five-kilowatt transmitters, the Voice of America maintains a relay base in Ceylon, whose signal may be heard all over South and Southeast Asia, especially in India, and as far west as Africa.

Banking

The Central Bank of Ceylon, which began operations in 1950, administers and regulates the monetary and banking system of the country. Its responsibilities are: to stabilize domestic monetary values; to preserve the par value of the rupee and to keep free its use for current international transactions; to promote and maintain a high level of production, employment, and real income in Ceylon; to encourage and promote the full development of the productive resources of Ceylon. The first Governor of the Central Bank was an American, John Exter, who helped the government set up the bank modelled partially on the Federal Reserve System of the United States. The Bank has the power of adjusting interest and discount rates, making changes in reserve requirements, and engaging in open market operations. Commercial banks are required by law to keep a minimum reserve with the Central Bank.

Commercial Banks perform the usual banking functions and finance Ceylon's import and export trade. All but one are branches of foreign banks (e.g., Chartered Bank; Hong Kong and Shanghai Banking Corporation). The Bank of Ceylon, which was established by the government in 1939, is the only Ceylonese commercial bank.

The Ceylon State Mortgage Bank, established in 1931, provides long-term credit for agricultural and other prescribed purposes.

The Agricultural and Industrial Credit Corporation, established in 1943, finances agricultural and industrial enterprises.

The Development Finance Corporation has already been described in the section on Agriculture.

Ceylon also has a small stock market, listing the stocks of nearly all tea and rubber companies and a number of industrial and commercial enterprises.

Trade

Ceylon's exports normally produce a favorable balance over imports. In the twenty years between 1936 and 1956 trade balances were favorable except in 1947, 1952, and 1953. The favorable balance of Rs. 478.9 million (about $101,000,000) in 1955, highest in Ceylon's history, however, fell to Rs. 101.3 million (about $22,000,000) in 1956 because of disadvantageous prices for the major exports, especially tea. In 1957, as the result of an increase in imports and continuing decline in the prices of tea and rubber, there was an unfavorable balance amounting to $26,000,000. In 1958, at the cost of overall economic activity and development and reduced imports, there was a favorable balance of more than $11,000,000.

Most of Ceylon's exports go to other Commonwealth countries, especially to the U.K., Australia, Canada, the Union of South Africa, and India. Among non-Commonwealth countries the largest share goes to the United States and the People's Republic of China. The United States, which buys about 8 percent of Ceylon's exports, is, after the U.K., Ceylon's best customer, though in 1957 China was in second place, ahead of the U.S.

Tea, rubber, and coconut products make up more than 95 percent of all of Ceylon's exports. The biggest buyers of tea are the U.K., the United States, Australia, the Union of South Africa, Iraq, Canada, and New Zealand. Best customers for rubber are China, the U.K., Western Germany, and the United States. Italy, Canada, the U.K., India, and the Netherlands buy most of the coconut oil. The U.K. and Western Germany take most of the desiccated coconut; India takes practically all the copra.

Ceylon's imports are mainly from Commonwealth countries. The non-Commonwealth countries from which Ceylon buys most are Burma, Communist China, and Japan. Imports from the United States account for approximately 4 percent of the total.

Food makes up more than 41 percent of Ceylon's imports, especially rice, wheat flour, and sugar. China supplied more than half the nearly 500,000 long tons of rice that the country needed in 1956 to supply her people's needs. Most of the remainder came from Burma. Wheat flour comes mainly from Australia and France, sugar from Cuba, Formosa, and Australia. Among other imports are motor fuels, oil, fertilizers, iron and steel, machinery, transport equipment, textiles, clothing, medicinal and pharmaceutical products, paper, tobacco, and coal.

Commercial Policy

In order to protect local industries and to regulate imports, Ceylon imposes import duties on several thousand items, giving preference to many of those shipped from Commonwealth countries. Export duties are also charged, especially on tea, rubber, and coconut products. More than half of all government revenue is derived from these duties.

As an international trader, Ceylon is a participant in the General Agreement on Tariffs and Trade and belongs to the International Monetary Fund and the International Bank for Reconstruction and Development. She is a member of the sterling area, to which in times of favorable trade balances she has contributed an appreciable number of dollars, retaining a part of them as an independent reserve in the Central Bank. Exchange control is maintained by the Central Bank, which limits dollar expenditures, restricting personal remittances and remittances for travel. The rupee, which was devalued in 1949 when the pound was devalued, is worth 4.76 to the dollar, 13.33 to the pound.

"Ceylonization" of trade, begun in 1949, extends to all forms of agricultural, industrial, and commercial exterprise, and is gradually shifting control of the country's resources from foreign to Ceylonese ownership and management.

Development Programs

In an effort to increase the country's production of food to keep pace with the growth in population, to decrease dependence on the three major export crops, whose future is uncertain, and to establish an economy which will be self-reliant without continued applications of foreign aid, the government of Ceylon has launched a number of economic development programs. The first was a six-year plan, inaugurated in 1948, which included projects to develop agriculture, irrigation, fisheries, industry, health, education, housing, and rural and village improvements. The most ambitious undertaking of this plan was the Gal-Oya multi-purpose project which will eventually provide irrigation for 100,000 acres reclaimed from virgin jungle, have a 25,000 kilowatt hydroelectric power station, make possible resettlement of 250,000 people in eastern Ceylon, and reduce the threat of flood damage such as brought widespread suffering in Ceylon during the summer of 1957.

The International Bank Mission recommended a new and more comprehensive plan for 1953–1959. Following many of the excellent proposals of this Mission, the government proposed a new six-year plan in 1954, calling for significant increase in expenditures for economic projects, including new attention to industry and to tourism. This plan never really got off the ground before the 1956 election, and under the Bandaranaike government a National Planning Council studied new plans. It set up a new ten-year plan to begin early in 1959, which would realistically deal with the country's financial needs and resources. By the end of 1958 the development programs of Ceylon were having serious difficulties.

Meanwhile, Ceylon has received substantial economic and technical assistance under the Colombo Plan and from a number of foreign countries. Between 1951 and 1958 other Commonwealth countries gave $23,250,000 in grants and loans to Ceylon. The United States was the largest source of aid up to 1958, having provided a total of $39,640,000 for agricultural assistance, irrigation, transportation, and education. In February, 1958, the USSR agreed to lend $30,000,000 to Ceylon at low interest rates to finance development projects and flood rehabilitation, and to provide technical assistance and training. Communist China in two aid agreements between 1957 and 1959 granted $15,750,000 for a rubber replanting program and $10,500,000 in a loan for flood rehabilitation. Even Czechoslovakia has loaned $3,420,000, and the International Bank and other United Nations agencies have loaned $24,370,000. Progress on Sino-Soviet aid projects was slow, and by the beginning of 1959 few projects had actually gone much beyond the planning stage. U.S. assistance programs, however, were well under way in 1958.

In addition to various aid programs under the International Cooperation Administration, the United States has donated milk and flour for the school lunch program, and sent emergency food supplies and substantial gifts of flour and food after the devastating floods of 1957.

Labor and Employment

Ceylonization has resulted in some labor difficulties since in the past the great body of workers came from India. Immigration from India has been serevely curtailed, and many Indian laborers have lost their residence permits. The International Bank Mission reported that both Ceylonese and foreign employers agree that the Sinhalese "is not naturally inclined toward hard physical labor," and that he prefers "a moderate pace with a minimum of physical exertion." Moreover, both Sinhalese and Ceylon Tamil workers normally choose to stay in the places where they were born. The supply of labor, then, is relatively immobile. Another reason for lack of flexibility among workers is the caste system, which still identifies some of the older occupations with certain castes.

Ceylonese workers are in general happy and easily satisfied. Except when they are aroused by agitators, they get along without demanding high wages, ideal working conditions, and special privileges if they think their employers are fair and sympathetic. They place a large premium on security, especially in government service, even at lower pay than they could get elsewhere. Quick to acquire skills, they have no driving ambition to rise out of steady, assured jobs. The International Bank Mission felt that the good nature and lack of aggressiveness of Ceylonese workmen and their unwillingness to move, keeping out of labor disputes, "may go far in aiding Ceylon's future industrial and economic development."

Unemployment, already becoming a serious problem, may well increase as the population grows. The Bank of Ceylon estimated in 1956 that out of a total labor force of 3,254,000, approximately 540,000 were totally unemployed and 386,000 severely underemployed.

Labor union activity is greater than is usual in underdeveloped economies. Several political leaders, especially of the three Communist groups, are identified with particular unions, often making use of strikes to advance political objectives. By 1958 half of the more than 600,000 plantations workers were organized, some of them in pro-Communist unions. 35,000 were in N. M. Perera's LSSP unions, which in 1958 controlled about 70 percent of urban labor, including the Port of Colombo and many government employees. The Communist Party controlled about 20 percent of urban labor, mainly workers in private commercial establishments and the articulate clerical group of government employees.

During 1957 and 1958, under a government favorable to labor, union activity increased. Only by substantial wage increases was the series of strikes which began in November of 1957 halted. These strikes, which affected even essential services, closed the Port of Colombo, and disrupted the tea and rubber market, seriously hurt the national economy.

Gross National Product

The decline in Ceylon's economy after 1956 is apparent in the drop in the Gross National Product from $1,049,000,000 in 1956 to $1,035,000,000 in 1957. The GNP in 1953 was only $928,000,000, with a per capita product of $114. The per capita product in 1957 was $113.

* * * * * * * * *

Ceylon is having a hard time economically. Like other young, underdeveloped countries, she is trying with commendable zeal to skip the tedious period of evolution from primitive methods to modern industrial dynamism. It is too early to estimate her probable success. Meanwhile, there are vexing and dangerous strains: tremendous population growth, decreased world demand for Ceylon's money-crops, failure of the country to be self-supporting, political unrest, labor troubles, floods and destruction of crops. The ambitious development projects, which will in time produce more food, clear land and irrigate it, diversify industry, and exploit natural resources, are very costly. Ceylon economists realize that the country must maintain its integrity by not becoming too dependent on foreign aid even though its own earning power is diminishing.

There is another, perhaps more serious problem than the straightforward one of finding food and room for an expanding population. That is the necessity of rapid cultural adjustment to the changes brought about by technological advances. The Ceylonese people are reluctant to change; they cling to old values and patterns of behavior. In a study of "Development Problems in Ceylon" made for the Institute of Pacific Relations in 1953, Burton Stein said that "if the technology which Ceylon is now attempting to absorb is to be assimilated, it may be necessary to take some cultural shortcuts." The Ceylonese people must become interested in hard work, he believes; they may have to resort to family planning; they must not resist new agricultural techniques. "The social engineering aspects of Ceylonese development will have to be pursued with the same energy as the technological aspects," he concludes, "or the fruits of the latter will be lost to the greatest number of Ceylonese."

Most thoughtful Ceylonese today agree with friendly

foreign observers that the success of Ceylon's development projects and her credit standing among the free nations of the world depend upon early settlement of communal quarrels and firm control of extremist elements.

6.   *The Religions of Ceylon*

The range of religious faiths among the various national or ethnic communities in Ceylon has already been noted. Most Sinhalese are Buddhists, most Tamils are Hindus, practically all Ceylon Moors and Malays are Muslims, Burghers are Christians, and so on. The government has published a fascinating list of religious groups, based on the report of the 1953 census:

Buddhists	5,209,439	64%
Hindus	1,610,561	19%
Muslims	541,506	6.5%
Christians	724,461	8.9%
Zoroastrians	1,295 ⎫	
Free Thinkers	1,750 ⎪	1.6%
Agnostics	865 ⎬	
Others	8,018 ⎭	

Here, with the exception of Judaism, are represented four of the major faiths of the world, some of the minor ones, and a proportionate share of the skeptics.

The Yakkhas and Nagas who, according to legend, inhabited Lanka before the coming of Vijaya, were demon and snake worshipers, primitive people who believed in good and evil spirits identified with the mysterious forces of nature. Some of their demons and their reverence for snakes, particularly the cobra, carried over into certain levels of the Hinduism and Buddhism that replaced animism. Or perhaps it would be more accurate to say that since all religions, no matter how highly developed, keep some of the vague fears, superstitions, and fetishes of primitive beginnings, the faiths of Ceylon are no exception. In Ceylon today there is still some belief in the efficacy of devil-dancing, exorcising wicked spirits that bring illness and misfortune. The cobra has sacred associations with Gautama Buddha, over whom in infancy a cobra raised its hood to shield him from the sun. Both Hindus and Buddhists believe that cobras are tutelary spirits and are very reluctant to kill them, however dangerous, allowing them to live in hollow trees or walls near their homes without molesting them.

Vijaya himself was a Brahman, who, however, broke caste rules by marrying a Yakkha princess. When Vijaya landed in Ceylon in 483 B.C., Siddhartha Gautama, the twenty-fifth Buddha, had just achieved

Nirvana. Like Vijaya, Gautama was a native of northern India. The two princes might possibly have known each other. The great world faith that grew up around Buddha did not come to Ceylon until the third century B.C., when Mahinda converted King Devanampiya Tissa. Meanwhile, under the tolerant rule of earlier Hindu kings, who followed the example of Vijaya, freedom of worship was established as a basic principle in Ceylon. Even during the reign of later devout Buddhist kings, Hinduism, animism, and even Christianity were allowed, and places of worship were provided.

Buddhism

Buddhism became the dominant religious faith of the island after King Tissa, and continues to be a powerful force in the daily lives of the Sinhalese today. Instead of being reabsorbed into Hinduism, as it was in the country of its origin, Buddhism in Ceylon remained strong, flexibly adjusting to Hinduism which threatened it, hospitably recognizing Hindu gods in its temples, developing as a great ethical creed of reason.

Not long after Buddhism was introduced into Ceylon, it began to decline in India as Brahman teachings replaced the tenets of Buddha. Gautama himself, like Christ, wrote nothing, and for several centuries after his death none of his teachings were written down. It was inevitable that Buddhist sects, each believing it followed the authentic interpretation of Buddha's words, should develop.

There are today four schools of Buddhism, each with subdivisions, all differing in many ways, all calling themselves the only true Buddhists. The oldest of these, and probably nearest to the original teaching, according to the English Buddhist scholar, Christmas Humphreys, is the *Theravada,* also known as the *Hinayana* ("little vehicle"). This is the religion of Ceylon, Burma, Thailand, Vietnam, Laos, and Cambodia. The second most important group which grew out of the early schisms in India, is called the *Mahayana* ("large vehicle"). It is the religion of Tibet, Nepal, China, Korea, and Japan, teaching the doctrine of salvation by faith and good works. Two sects of *Mahayana* have important enough differences to be regarded as schools in their own right. These are Tibetan Buddhism, which extends to Bhutan and Sikkim, and the Zen Buddhism of Japan. The somewhat invidious names, *Mahayana* and *Hinayana,* were invented by the Mahayanists, who, in Humphreys's words, "claimed that theirs was a career or course of life large enough to bear all mankind to salvation; the Hinayanists called themselves the Theravadins, followers of the Doctrine of the Elders, and claimed to teach the Buddha-way as pointed out by the Master."

Buddhism, strictly speaking, is a philosophy or ethical concept of life rather than a religion. Buddha was a teacher, not a god, and claimed no divinity, though some of his followers worship him as if he were divine. The teachings of Buddha, which are the life study of many learned men in many countries, may be much too simply summarized as man's need to eliminate desire by following the "Eightfold Path" to truth: right faith, right aspiration, right action, right speech, right effort, right mode of living, right attention, and right meditation. Until he achieves complete freedom from passion, hatred and delusion, man must be born over and over again into miserable life. The final goal is *Nirvana* or *Nibbana,* which is complete detachment from worldliness, total extinction of physical being. One who attains *Nirvana* can do so only through contemplation; only then is he "enlightened."

This explanation fails to take into account the many intricacies of a highly intellectualized body of doctrine or to differentiate among the various Buddhist dogmas. In general, Buddhists are forbidden to kill, to steal, to lie, to commit adultery, or to become drunk. They are enjoined to be pure, patient, and brave, to give alms generously, and to seek knowledge. The *bhikkus* or monks are not clergymen in the usual sense, but men who undertake lives of austerity in order to attain *Nirvana.* They must not eat after mid-day, sing or dance, wear ornaments of any kind, sleep on comfortable beds, or otherwise indulge in luxuries. They own

174

nothing but their saffron-colored robes, their fans, razors, needles, umbrellas, and begging bowls.

Buddhism in Ceylon today is still vigorous, though some of its practitioners seem to be more interested in the political than the spiritual aspects of their religion. A number of its leaders would like to see Buddhism the dominant power in the state, as it was under the Sinhalese kings, when high-ranking monks served as royal advisors. In 1956, many of the *bhikkus* took active part in the elections, advancing such causes as the Sinhalese Only language law, the adoption of traditional dress, and the increased support of monasteries and Buddhist schools. The presence of monks on political platforms and other participation in secular activity are deplored by conservative Buddhists, who feel that their gentle, contemplative faith is being corrupted by behavior unsanctioned in Lord Buddha's teachings.

Whatever the effect on the purity of Theravadic Buddhism of recent developments among the *Sangha* (the monastic order) in Ceylon, there is little change in the piety of the average Sinhalese. He happily gives food and alms to every *bhikku* who presents his begging bowl, keeps votive lamps lighted under the sacred Bo-trees, practices the prescribed fast and abstinence on the four quarter days of the moon, attends services and places bouquets of frangipani and jasmine and other flowers in the temples, cheerfully goes on pilgrimages under the most trying circumstances, takes part in the frequent festivals in honor of Buddhist holy days, particularly on full-moon day, the most important time of the month.

The visitor to Ceylon who really wants to understand the Ceylonese people would do well to make the difficult pilgrimage to the top of Adam's Peak, which is called Sri Pada (The Sacred Footprint) by the Sinhalese. This mountain has for centuries been venerated by Buddhists, Hindus, Muslims, and Christians. On the summit is a great boulder in which is a footprint-shaped depression. Buddhists believe that it is the mark of the foot of Buddha, who stood there on his third visit, in the eighth year of his Buddhahood, not long before Vijaya landed in Ceylon. The Hindus believe it is the mark of Siva. The Christians and Muslims say it is the footprint of Adam, obliged to stand for a thousand years on one foot after being expelled from the Garden of Eden. Another Christian legend is that the footprint was made by St. Thomas, the Doubter, who visited Ceylon during his residence in India.

To the Peak each year go thousands of devout Buddhist pilgrims, paying homage to what is to them, next to the Tooth Relic, their most sacred object of worship. The best time for the climb is between December and April, before the rainy season. The starting-place is Hatton, which can be reached by train. From there a bus or taxi takes the pilgrim to Laksapana, at the foot of the peak. The climb of eight miles, up the very steep mountain, is most comfortably made during the night, in the coolness before the rising of the fierce tropical sun that scorches even on the high slopes during the day. At the time that Ibn Batuta and Marco Polo climbed Adam's Peak and, indeed, up to 1950, the trail had to be lighted by torches carried by the pilgrims themselves. Now, a line of electric lights creeps up the steep trail, all the way to the temple on the summit. They were placed there in fulfillment of a vow made to Sri Sumana, tutelary god of the mountain, by Sir John Kotelawala, at that time Minister of Transport and Works, on the successful launching of the first major hydroelectric scheme in Ceylon.

The foreigner who wants to climb Sri Pada must not approach it as if it were just another peak to be mastered by a hardy hiker. He must have some of the patience and spiritual exaltation that mark the true pilgrims. If he barges up, shouldering aside the slower climbers, paying no attention to the demonstration of reverence, unselfish consideration of others, and fortitude that may be seen on every side, dismissing the motivation of his fellow-climbers as superstition, he will learn nothing about Ceylon. He'd be better off flexing his muscles in the Rockies or the Alps or on the beach at Colombo's Mount Lavinia. But if he is aware of the brotherhood of man and is sensitive to the sympathy that kindles among good people doing a good thing, his experience should be a rewarding one.

During the season thousands of pilgrims are on the mountain every night, especially on full-moon nights. Many of them have come long distances, often from other Buddhist countries, to gain spiritual merit from visiting Sri Pada. They are usually bare-footed, in thin cotton clothing, suitable for the heat of lowland Ceylon, but not for the cold winds of dawn nearly a mile and a half above sea-level. Their diet is low in proteins, and they are not a robust people. Yet without a murmur of complaint, the pilgrims climb a trail which is essentially an eight-mile staircase whose steps are of uneven height, hewn from the rocky side of the mountain, formidable enough to tire healthy western athletes in strong shoes and proper clothing. Some of them are so eager that their families should earn the merit of the pilgrimage that they carry children and support aged and ailing relatives up the long trail. In double bags over their shoulders they take clean clothing, food for the journey, and offerings of flowers and money for the temple. So they travel slowly, crippled and whole, young and old, inspired by the joyful purpose of their journey, which may take many days. As they toil up the jagged stairs, they chant the hymns of Buddhism, with frequent interjections of the word "Saddhu!" which roughly corresponds to "Hallelujah!" No one is impatient, even when the trail narrows to a single stairway up, separated by an iron railing from a single line down, straight into the sky above the timberline, and the long line of pilgrims slows to a crawl. The Westerner who joins them in their devotion to the Sacred Footprint is welcome indeed. He will never be closer to the warm, friendly heart of the Ceylonese people.

On top, each pilgrim may ring a bell at the entrance to the temple, once for every time he has climbed Sri Pada. Then he files slowly past the footprint, in which priests press lengths of cloth brought up by the faithful for this extraordinary blessing, makes his offering (for which there is absolutely no solicitation), and goes to the eastern parapet to watch for the dawn. As the sky lightens, the deep, misty valleys and the rugged outlines of neighboring mountains gradually appear and the sinuous line of electric lights, that goes down the rocky cliff into the forest far below, dims. Suddenly the sun punctures the rosy horizon as a great cry of adoration and rapture rises from the watchers. On the western side, staying for an eerie minute or two, the shadow of the pyramid-shaped peak stands across the sky and the murky ridges and valleys. The phenomenon of the Shadow of the Peak is one of the wonders of Ceylon. But far more worth the hard climb is the assurance of human understanding, regardless of creed.

Another remarkable example of Buddhist worship is the annual *Esala Perahera,* the August procession in honor of the Tooth Relic, probably the most colorful and enchanting parade in the world. Each night and one afternoon for ten days at the time of the August full moon, the Relic is carried in a jeweled casket on the back of a resplendently decorated royal tusker about the streets of Kandy, the ancient capital of the highland Sinhalese. Escorting the Temple elephant are upwards of a hundred other panoplied elephants, brought in from the estates of Sinhalese chiefs and from other temples, many troupes of Kandyan dancers, performing the vigorous, masculine, traditional dances of Ceylon, jugglers, dancing boys, torch-bearers, whip-crackers (to clear the roads), Kandyan aristocrats in flat, square gold hats and gold shoes, padded about their middles with many yards of cloth—over which are brocaded jackets and sashes holding short swords—, relic-bearing palanquins, even mobile generators providing the modern touch of electric lights on the trappings of some of the elephants.

This brilliant procession, watched with sincere reverence by orderly crowds, is a spectacle never to be forgotten. It begins and ends in the courtyard of the famous *Dalada Maligawa,* the Temple of the Tooth, a thick-walled building, surrounded by a moat in which swim scores of large turtles. Along the line of march the dancers, wearing many-ruffled sarongs, silver belts like sporrans, and conical silver hats on wide brims, tell their stories in great, angular, spread-legged leaps, describing such things as the horse on which Prince

Siddhartha rode off as he renounced the world, the seduction of the Yakkha princess by Vijaya, tragic death, triumphant joy. Kandyan dancing, religious in origin, is a splendid, age-old expression of exuberance and strength. With the dancers are drummers, beating out tireless rhythms, *pantheru* (tambourine) bearers, fire-jugglers, flute players. In and out of the procession roll carts full of copra, with which attendants replenish the flaming braziers on long poles, spilling puddles of fire into the street, around which the barefoot dancers must carefully maneuver. Meanwhile, the great Temple tusker walks in stately dignity on long white cloths which are hurriedly gathered up behind him as he goes with his precious burden, to be laid down again in front of him. His trunk, like that of all the other well-behaved elephants in the *Perahera,* is curled under his mouth in the attitude of respect.

Hinduism

Hinduism in Ceylon is practically identical with that in south India, holding to the traditions of Indian ceremonials and customs. Some Ceylonese Hindus, according to the Tamil writer, A. M. K. Cumaraswamy, profess a philosophical faith which has some affinity with Buddhism, except that it rejects what he calls the Buddhist "position of practical atheism." For the most part, however, the Tamils are conservative followers of Siva, whom they worship as the Supreme Deity rather than as the Destroyer in the Hindu trinity of Brahma, the Creator, who has no temples in Ceylon, and Vishnu, the Preserver, who has a few temples. Siva and his consort Parvati are worshiped together in the many temples dedicated to him, and their sons, Ganesh, the elephant-headed god, and Skanda, or Subramanya, are very popular.

The basic tenets of Hinduism are: belief in the authority of the sacred scriptures known as the Vedas, in the immortality of the soul, which in Cumaraswamy's words, is "an independent entity with a timeless origin and an eternal destiny," in the existence of a Supreme Being, in the theory of re-birth, in reverence for ancestors, in the social pattern of four major castes, and in the four paths to heaven. These are the path of ritual and ceremonial observances, which includes consultation with priests, astrologers, and wise men; the path of virtuous conduct, which includes unselfish generosity, atonement for wrong-doing, abstinence from both evil and pleasure; the path of devotion and meditation, including prayers, pilgrimages, self-discipline, even asceticism; the path "of the enlightened soul who sees things in correct perspective, and whose spiritual discernment enables him to go through life with imperturbable placidity, with the confidence of one who has found his moorings, and who knows he is on his way to his right home."

The devout Buddhist and the devout Hindu are

likely to be good people, both deeply concerned with *karma*, which is the inexorable influence on future existence of one's deeds in this life, part of the cycle of incarnation leading to *Nirvana*, the final sublimation for both. Some of the splendid traditions of both faiths: close family relationships, deference of children to their parents, habits of contemplation, rigorous rules of physical discipline, temperance, chastity, and tolerance of others' ideas and beliefs—have weakened, perhaps because of Western influences. For the most part, however, they still prevail, especially outside of the cities.

The visitor to Ceylon interested in religious practices may visit the jungle shrine of Kataragama, in southeastern Ceylon, at the time of the annual fire-walking ceremonies in July or August, depending on the moon. Kataragama is a place of pilgrimage especially important to Hindus, though Buddhists too pay homage to the god of Kataragama, Skanda, the son of Siva and Parvati, god of war, sometimes called Subramanya or, in India, Kartikeya. The story of Kataragama may be found in an excellent short novel about Ceylon, Leonard Woolf's *A Village in the Jungle*.

To Kataragama go thousands of pilgrims in fulfillment of vows, some to bathe in the sacred river or to offer gifts to the temples, others to torture their flesh by thrusting skewers through their cheeks and tongues and hooks through the skin of their backs and chests, or to roll in the dust around the temple in fulfillment of vows and atonement for their sins, or on the night of the fire-walking to prove their faith by walking barefooted over a pit of flaming coals.

Compared with the serene exaltation of the pilgrimage to Sri Pada, Kataragama is sensational and to some tastes barbaric. It should not be regarded as typical of Hindu worship, which can be as spiritually elevated as that of the Buddhists. The *Deepavali* Festival, around November, sometimes called the Festival of the Lights, and the *Vel* Festival, in July or August, which features street mumming and processions with elaborately decorated carts, better demonstrate the poetic beauty and the essential place of religion in the lives of Ceylon's Hindus.

Hindu temples are usually very ornate, their facades covered with brightly colored images of the many gods of Hindu theology. They are in strong contrast to the simple, even stark Buddhist temples, usually built near the characteristic bell-shaped white *dagobas*. Buddhist temples often house heroic figures of the Buddha and flat, formalized wall paintings of events in the Master's life. Into many of the Buddhist temples have moved some of the more attractive Hindu deities, who are honored along with the Lord Buddha. This relationship is not altogether surprising if we remember that Buddhism was originally an offshoot of Hinduism, and that in Ceylon the two religions have coexisted for over two thousand years, sometimes with the Tamil Hindus dominant.

Other Faiths

Ceylon Muslims follow the laws of Islam, wearing fezzes, offering prayers five times a day, facing in the direction of Mecca (which, of course is to the northwest rather than to the east), keeping the thirty-day fast of Ramazan, making the pilgrimage to Mecca if they can afford it, and taking care of their poor. They have their own schools and mosques and form a substantial, prosperous, God-fearing part of the population.

The Christians, outnumbering the Muslims, make up about 9 percent of all Ceylonese. The Catholics, strong in the faith which came to Ceylon with the Portuguese and survived the Dutch and British regimes, are the largest group, with its spiritual head the Archbishop of Colombo. Many of the Protestants are Jaffna Tamils converted by American missionaries, though there are also members of the Dutch Reformed Church and a considerable number of members of the Church of England, who became Christians under the British. Christian missionaries are still active in many parts of the island, carrying on the work of the Catholic Franciscans, who came first in 1506, followed by the Jesuits, Augustinians, and Dominicans; the Baptists, who came in 1812; the Methodists, who came in

1814; and the American Congregationalists, who came in 1816, founding Jaffna College and other schools and medical missions in northern Ceylon.

Religious Holidays

Ceylon's traditional, many-sided, tolerant attitude towards religion is indicated in the large numbers of religious holidays officially celebrated each year. The dates are approximate, varying with the lunar cycle.

January: Hindu *Thai Pongal,* in honor of the god of the sun, Suriya.

March, April: Christian Easter.

May: Buddhist *Wesak:* the celebration of Buddha's birthday, his attainment of Buddhahood, and his death.

Variable: Muslim end of *Ramazan* (9th month of lunar year).

July, August: Hindu *Vel* Festival, celebrating the triumph of the god Kanadasamy over the forces of evil.

September, October: Muslim *Hadji* Festival.

October, November: Hindu *Deepavali* Festival.

At varying times, usually in December, January: The Prophet *Mahomet's* birthday.

December 25: Christmas.

A Break with Tradition

The communal uprisings of 1958, though basically economic, had in them an element of religious fanaticism. The gentle faith of Buddha was distorted by a few extremists, who may have been egged on by subversive alien influence, to rise against all non-Buddhist

186

groups, particularly the Hindus. Their latent hostility aroused, along with their instinct for self-preservation, some of the Hindus and Christians retaliated with the same savage violence. With order restored, the sensible Ceylonese are trying once again to live together in the spirit of tolerance that has characterized both the Buddhists and the Hindus in the past. It is still too early to determine the historical significance—or even to understand all the causes—of these unhappy events. The breach between the two groups, however, is a serious one.

187

7. The Arts of Ceylon: Past and Present

Though contemporary artistic trends in Ceylon are interesting, no work of worldwide distinction has been produced in modern times. Ceylonese literature is still in a formative stage; there is no professional Ceylonese theatre. Kandyan dancing, which has come down from centuries of dancing in connection with Buddhist temple ceremonies, is not likely to have influence elsewhere on the dance as an art form. Only in painting is the tradition an important one, which is being carried on by a group of talented painters, chief among them the internationally known George Keyt.

In the past, however, Ceylon has been the home of vital and enduring art. The remains of this art are evident in many parts of the country, in the architecture of ruined temples and palaces, in the frescoes on the walls and ceilings of caves, and, most remarkable, in the exposed niches of Sigiriya, in the stone carvings of the old temples, in the great *dagobas* themselves, in the temple libraries and treasure-rooms. The highly developed Sinhalese civilization began to decline long before the coming of Europeans, who did little to encourage indigenous art. Only the folk arts, such as work in silver and copper and lacquer and the setting of gems and the *Kolam* masks of the south of Ceylon, have survived through the hundreds of years of European domination.

Independence has been accompanied by a revival of interest in Sinhalese art and writing, and there is tremendous pride in the cultural masterpieces of the past. Contemporary intellectual and cultural activity is not yet strongly rooted in that great past; it is seeking its own way among both Western and Eastern influences, having lost its continuity partly because of the superposition of European values, partly because of the inexorable forces of decadence which halted the production of great works of art after Parakrama Bahu.

Though we speak of the ancient art of Ceylon as Sinhalese, it had its origins in the art of India. The Tamil invaders brought with them their artists and builders, but except for obvious Indian influence on the architecture and sculpture of Polonnaruwa, little remains today of their direct contribution to the arts. What we call Sinhalese art was in the beginning a blend of Indian concepts of religious imagery and indigenous Sinhalese genius. Martin Wickramasinghe, in his book, *Aspects of Sinhalese Culture,* admits that "the Sinhalese borrowed many cultural elements from India. But the borrowed elements changed in the process of adaptation," and he points out that the borrowing was not from Hindu India, but from Buddhist India.

Scholars will probably never agree about the extent to which the culture of Ceylon is derived from that of India. Some have even tried to trace it back through India to Persia and Hellenistic Asia Minor. Others, like the distinguished Ceylon Tamil scholar, Dr. Ananda Coomaraswamy, who served for thirty years as Research Fellow in Indian, Iranian, and Mohammedan art at the Boston Museum of Fine Arts, have believed that the art of Ceylon was distinctly Indian, without influence from Greece or Rome, and that, maturing independently, it exerted influence on the splendid Gupta art of India (320–535 A.D.) and became the model for the Buddhist art which spread eastward from Ceylon. The patriotic Sinhalese view is expressed by Professor G. P. Malalasekera, Professor of Pali at the University of Ceylon, appointed Ambassador to Soviet Russia in 1956:

We have not made sufficient boast yet of the fact that here we have in Lanka, in our temples, a religious art second to none in the world, and what is even more remarkable, with an unbroken continuity stretching over the centuries, a continuity that can be traced *from extant records* with a certainty almost unparalleled in any other single country. Time was when critics, some of them, alas! of our own race, revelled in saying that all our achievements in art were the results of Indian influence. More and more it is being revealed that it is just as much likely that, as far as Buddhist art is concerned, the reverse was the case. Whatever might be the ultimate results of these rival claims, there is not the slightest doubt that everywhere in the continent of Asia there is a strong similarity of technique in the portrayal of Buddhist subjects manifesting itself in all sorts of ways, and till we have convincing reasons for the contrary view, Lanka might well be regarded as having set the fashions which were adopted in other Buddhist lands.

Visitors to the ruined cities, to the cave temples of Dambulla, and to other relics of the past, some of which may also be seen in the museums of Colombo and Kandy, soon realize that the ancient art of Ceylon is almost entirely religious in theme. Except for the sensuous figures in the Sigiriya frescoes, the painting as well as the architecture was dedicated to Buddhism during the ascendancy of the Sinhalese Kings (though not, of course, during the periods of Hindu domination). The arts were either under the patronage of the kings or of the Buddhist clergy, both of whom were interested in temple construction and decoration. The greatest of the Sinhalese kings, it will be remembered, were those who built many splendid shrines and temples. Artists were often attached to the courts and temples, in caste relationship, giving their services in exchange for land and protection. Even today, some craftsmen and artists, as well as dancers, are associated with certain temples, especially in Kandy. This religious influence on the arts, though immensely productive, has tended to inhibit the development of a secular culture.

The Ceylon Tamils have not produced an art and literature of their own outside of the main body of Tamil intellectual activity which has its center in Madras. Other racial groups, who came much later and whose interests were for the most part in trade and exploitation, have contributed little to the arts of Ceylon.

Architecture

The earliest buildings, which were made of wood, have entirely disappeared, except for stone stairways and pillars, which may be seen in the parts of Anuradhapura now cleared of jungle. Some temples were made of stone, whose workmanship reached a high point of excellence and good taste during the ninth and tenth centuries. The principal construction material, however, was brick, which was used extensively in the *dagobas,* many of which were of solid brick, and in nearly all other important buildings. As lime became known, it was used to face the walls of brick temples and to cover the massive vaulting. The *dagobas* were also coated with lime, giving them a smooth, hard surface which protected them from the weather and the inroads of jungle vegetation.

The first of the major *dagobas* was the Thuperama, built in Anuradhapura in 307 B.C. by King Tissa after his conversion to Buddhism. It has been restored and may be seen today, a gleaming white, bell-shaped structure, on which is the usual conical spire, topped by a gilded finial. This *dagoba,* like many others, is surrounded by many slender monolithic pillars which may once have been covered to form a kind of arcade. This lovely shrine, which contains the collarbone of Buddha in a small sealed chamber inside the square base of the spire, is said to be the oldest surviving building in either India or Ceylon.

The biggest of the Anuradhapura *dagobas,* the Abhayagiri, now in ruins and covered with trees and bushes, was built in the 2nd century B.C. by one of the successors to the noble Dutthagamini, who wanted to surpass the great construction of Dutthagamini's reign. The Abhayagiri was larger than all the Pyramids of Egypt except one. It is estimated to have contained twenty million cubic feet of brick, enough to build a wall ten feet high and one foot thick from London to Edinburgh. Its original height was 450 feet, higher than St. Paul's Cathedral, and its dome was 360 feet in diameter. Its base covered eight acres.

Most striking of the *dagobas* in Anuradhapura to-day is the beautiful, fully restored Ruanweli, whose gilded tip may be seen for miles above the surrounding jungles. Around the platform which circles the base of this *dagoba,* above a paved road which once carried mighty processions, is a wall of elephant heads which seem to support a higher platform. These heads, made of brick which was covered with lime and painted, are nine feet high. There are four hundred of them, all of which once had tusks of ivory.

At Anuradhapura little remains of the once magnificent city except the restored *dagobas* and the fascinating mounds still proudly topped by the square platforms and tapering spires, which have lost their battle with the forces of decay and the fecundity of the jungle. There are also stone baths, fallen pillars, some pieces of sculpture, and the remains of a few buildings, including the 1600 stone pillars that once supported the nine-story Brazen Palace of Dutthagamini.

In far better preservation are the temples and palaces of Polonnaruwa, built over a thousand years after the golden age of Anuradhapura, especially during the thirty-three-year reign of the great Sinhalese king, Parakrama Bahu, in the twelfth century. There the tourist with an interest in archaeology, architecture, or art may wander for days in a splendid outdoor museum. Polonnaruwa, which was the capital of the Tamils as well as the Sinhalese, shows very plainly the handiwork of Hindu artists. For example, the Lankatilake (sometimes called the Jetawanarama) was a temple to Buddha in mixed Indian and Sinhalese styles. It is a tremendous structure, built of brick, whose vaulted roof has fallen in, leaving exposed a headless standing statue of Buddha which must have been at least sixty feet high. The walls, covered with figures in relief, are twelve feet thick. Another remarkable building is known as the Vatadage, a round temple built on two terraces, one above the other. From the lower terrace four wonderfully wrought stairways at the cardinal points of the compass lead to the upper platform, in the center of which is a small *dagoba* with four seated Buddhas, carved from stone, facing the entrances. The now roofless brick walls rise twenty feet above the platform. Before the Buddhas each day are placed fresh offerings of incense and flowers, brought by devout villagers, who walk long distances to this still sacred shrine.

It is a curious fact that the only ancient buildings in Ceylon built entirely of stone were Hindu temples, such as may be seen in Polonnaruwa. Stone was used by the Sinhalese, but mainly for the bases, doorways, pillars, and stairways of wooden buildings. Roofs were made of timber covered with tiles. After the eleventh century, the buildings were almost entirely constructed of bricks, plastered with lime. One of the best preserved examples of this type of construction is the Lankatilake temple near Kandy, built in the 14th century, very oriental in appearance, an interesting variation of later Kandyan architecture.

After Parakrama Bahu the Great and his immediate successors, there was little interest in or talent for building big new shrines. Under the European invaders the great arts of stonework and brickwork were nearly forgotten, and the marvelous temples, pavilions, and palaces fell into decay. The jungle covered Anuradhapura and Polonnaruwa as the capital shifted from city to city farther south, out of the Dry Zone.

The Dutch introduced their own characteristic styles into the churches and dwellings of Colombo, which was built as a Western city. Their solid buildings were relieved by ornamental fanlights over the lintels of doorways and by quaint Dutch medieval gables such as may be seen today in the Dutch churches of Colombo, Jaffna, and Galle. Their houses, which set the pattern for many of the luxurious bungalows of Colombo, had front porticos and verandahs, central halls, and central courtyards.

Sculpture

The hardness of the stone of Ceylon, gneiss, which is like granite, probably accounts for the relatively small amount of work done in stone, including sculpture. There are, however, some very charming examples of Buddhist art in the bas-reliefs of the Anuradhapura period and some fine pieces of sculpture in the round after the tenth century. Critics do not assign a very high place to early Ceylonese sculpture in comparison with the great art of the Greeks, but it has its own excellence and originality and is in no way inferior to the somewhat similar sculpture of India of the same period. Indeed it has a freshness and seeming newness, the result of slow wearing, that give it extraordinary interest.

The most delightful examples of the early Buddhist sculpture are the "moonstones," which are found nowhere else in the world. They are semicircular stones at the foot of stairways, carved in low relief in concentric lines of animals, lotus-flowers, and birds. Often the outer circle has the four animals most highly honored in Ceylon: the horse, the bull, the elephant, and the lion, which are associated with the four quarters of the moon. There is also, usually, one ring of sacred geese. Connoisseurs of art are deeply impressed by the best of these Anuradhapura moonstones, for the conception is vigorous and imaginative, and the carving is masterful.

The moonstones are often found in conjunction with guardstones, round-topped stones about three to three and a half feet high, fifteen inches wide, and nine inches deep, in which figures of kings, dancers, dwarfs, and the like are carved in high relief. These stones, one on each side, "guard" the stairways. The stone risers of the steps are sometimes carved with marvelous little figures of dwarfs, in constantly varied positions, all with mobile, good-natured faces, who seem to be holding up the stairs. These dwarfs, called *Bahiravayas,* are among the most captivating of all Sinhalese art forms. They may also be found on the stone pillar capitals in Anuradhapura, in attitudes of dancing and playing, and on the walls of the Polonnaruwa temples, grinning and grimacing. The happy, laughing, grotesque figures of Ceylon's sculptured dwarfs throw an interesting sidelight on the Sinhalese sense of humor. Most admired of other sculpture found in Anuradhapura is the small charming relief, called "The Lovers," from Isurumuniya, a rock temple near a crocodile-haunted lotus pond.

In the Polonnaruwa period the taste for the small, delicate carving of Anuradhapura had changed to a fondness for the colossal. Huge Buddhas, made from bricks and plastered, such as are still being built in modern temples, or carved out of the living rock, became fashionable. The most notable of the rock sculptures are those at Galvihara, carved during the reign of Parakrama Bahu the Great. There are three figures, one lying on its side, forty-four feet in length, another standing, twenty-two feet high, and a third, on a smaller scale, less majestic than the others, in the familiar cross-legged seated position of many statues of Buddha. The standing figure is thought to be that of the disciple Ananda, mourning over the dead Buddha, who had achieved *Nirvana,* lying at his feet. This group, hewn from one immense boulder, is impressive indeed, especially the standing figure, a masterpiece of gently stylized sorrow, the arms crossed on the chest, the earlobes pierced and curiously elongated.

Another fine example of heroic rock sculpture is the naturalistic figure of a man holding what is supposed to be an *ola* manuscript, not far from the shore of the great Topaweva, one of the ancient irrigation tanks at Polonnaruwa. This statue is popularly believed to be a portrait statue of the mustached, dignified Parakrama Bahu. But scholars now say that it represents either a Hindu religious teacher or a legendary Indian wise man named Agastya.

Painting

After Buddhism became established in Ceylon, artists came from India, sent by King Asoka, to depict the life of Buddha. Early Buddhist art, as Ananda Coomaraswamy has pointed out, was "popular, sensuous, animistic Indian art adapted to the purpose of the illustration of Buddhist anecdote and the decoration of the Buddhist monuments." In Ceylon it soon became formalized and metaphysical and then, as it

was influenced by Hindu theism, new interest in romantic form produced sculpture and painting far removed from the earlier ascetic art.

Very early in this artistic progression, oil may have
been used in painting. *The Mahavamsa* mentions the
use of oil mixed with pigments in the fourth century
B.C., earlier than in any other country. There is some
evidence that some of the buildings of the Polonnaruwa
period and probably earlier were colored with oil
paint (though Coomaraswamy doubts that oil was ever
used in the early period). The paintings on the walls
of cave-temples and brick structures which have survived were done in tempera, yolk of egg in some kind
of solution with pigments, applied to wet plaster.

Most famous of the fresco paintings are those at
Sigiriya, executed near the end of the fifth century
A.D. The twenty-one paintings that still remain of
the original five hundred "golden-colored ones" may
be seen today in two chambers of a shallow cave at
Sigiriya about forty feet above the base of the west
face of the rock. For many centuries the cave was ac-
cessible only by ladders; today a narrow iron spiral
staircase rises to the home of the Sigiriya ladies. According to Senarat Paranavitana, the Ceylonese archae-
ologist, who wrote a brilliant introduction to the
UNESCO-sponsored book, *Ceylon Paintings from Temple, Shrine, and Rock,* the unknown artist prepared
the rough rock surface by plastering it with liver-red

alluvium reinforced with vegetable fibers and rice husks. Over this went a buff-colored composition containing sand, clay, lime, and vegetable fibers. The uppermost layer, one-eighth inch thick, was composed of sand and lime mortar, smoothed, then covered with pure lime. The entire plaster was from three-eighths of an inch to an inch thick.

The ladies, in pairs, one fairer skinned than the other, apparently her servant, were painted in glowing red, yellow, green, black, and white, but no blue. The figures are variously supposed to be beauties of King Kasyapa's court, carrying flowers to a temple, or what Paranavitana calls "cloud damsels, lightning princesses," in clouds which cut them off at the waist. Coomaraswamy thought they were goddesses since divine beings are generally represented at half-length, hidden from the waist down by conventional clouds. But whether divine or human, the voluptuous ladies have fascinated lovers of the female form for fifteen hundred years. Though the princesses seem to be bare-breasted, they are actually wearing diaphanous blouses. Their head-dresses and jewelry are rich and varied. The attendant girls are more modestly attired.

The Sigiriya frescoes are contemporary with and superficially resemble those in the Ajanta Caves in India. Paranavitana, however, points out the considerable differences between Sigiriya and Ajanta, saying that the artists of Sigiriya "shared the ideals of the

Indian painters, but their treatment of the feminine form differed in detail." The Sigiriya figures, narrow of hip and long in the waist, show the "conscious gravity" of the Sinhalese, as opposed to the "gay exuberance" of the short-waisted, big-hipped Indian women. This interpretation of Indian joyousness and Sinhalese seriousness does not square with the usual analysis of the difference between the Sinhalese and the Indians, but it may have been true at the time of the paintings. Certainly Kasyapa's women had little reason to be gay. In any event, the painters of Sigiriya had no influence on later Sinhalese art, though some modern Ceylonese painters have attempted a style reminiscent of Sigiriya.

Next in importance to the Sigiriya frescoes are the wall-paintings, depicting scenes from the life of Buddha, in the Tivanka shrine in Polonnaruwa. Others, showing such historical scenes as the landing of Vijaya and the duel between Dutthagamini and Elara, are on the walls of the rock temple at Dambulla.

There was little painting of consequence after the twelfth century, though in the eighteenth century and later, new Buddhist temples were built, lavishly decorated with religious scenes, painted in an ornate, colorful style that lacks the genius of the earlier painting. Ceylonese painting in its period of distinction, unquestionably a lineal descendant of Indian painting, developed its own characteristic style that kept its vitality after Indian painting declined. Coomaraswamy says that "Sinhalese art is of particular value as preserving early Hindu feeling which in most parts of the mainland has been obscured by Muhammadan or later Hindu motifs. Sinhalese decorative art is thus in a sense both freer and wider than that of Northern India in later times, and gentler, less grotesque, more akin to mediaeval European, than the Dravidian art of Southern India, to which it is, nevertheless, so closely related."

There is still in Ceylon today a serious interest in painting, much of it strongly influenced by Western styles, but some of it, particularly that of George Keyt in his most vital period, seeking inspiration in traditional Sinhalese art, interpreted in modern terms. Keyt is one of a group of artists, called the " '43 Group," which in 1943 boldly attempted to create an artistic renaissance in Ceylon. Best known of these artists are Keyt, Harry Pieris, and Justin Deraniyagala.

Music

Music, except as rhythmic accompaniment to dancing, mainly percussive, has never reached a high stage of development among the Sinhalese. The Tamils, on the other hand, have always been a very musical people. Hindu teachers encourage the study of music, whose origin they trace back to the Vedas. The god Siva is often represented as a musician and dancer, and the wife of Brahma, Sarasvati, is the goddess of music. Narada, the son of Brahma and Sarasvati, is believed to have invented the *vina,* the very popular Indian seven-stringed instrument with two gourd resonance chambers. Both music and dancing were studied in India from the very earliest known period, and in both Saivite and Vaishnite temples music plays an important part in the services.

The music of south India, called Karnatic, was brought to Ceylon by the Tamils, and it has generally followed the development in India without greatly influencing the Sinhalese. Karnatic music is a purely melodic art without harmonized accompaniment. It is expressed in six basic combinations of sounds called *ragas,* which have come down from antiquity, to which are added other melodies. Among the stringed instruments, which are preferred to wind instruments, are the *vina,* the *sitar,* similar to the *vina,* and the *sarangi,* played with a bow like a violin. Flutes, the *nagasvara,* a kind of clarinet, and the *pongi,* which has only one note, are the wind instruments. Drums of various types and small cymbals and gongs are also used in the "oriental" orchestras, which are becoming increasingly popular in Ceylon today, even among the Sinhalese, partly in protest against the spread of Western music.

The music of the early Sinhalese, according to Tennent, "consisted of sound rather than of harmony; modulation and expression having been at all times subordinate to volume and metrical effect." Temple music consisted chiefly of the beating of drums, of which there were more than thirty varieties. Tennent, who listened with an Englishman's distaste for most Eastern music, says that in his day harmony was still subordinate to noise, and that the music of the temples, made by flutes, *chanks* (a kind of horn made from shells), and tom-toms, was nearly overpowering. He compared the singing of the Sinhalese, "a nasal whine," to that of the Arabs. Many Westerners are inclined to agree with Tennent, not being able to follow Coomaraswamy's advice to "forget all implied harmonies" and "recover the sense of pure intonation." There is, however, increasing interest among European and American lovers of music in the *ragas* and improvisations of Asian music, which have already had some influence on Western composers.

One of Ceylon's fine artists, Devar Surya Sena, disagrees with the opinions of Tennent and other European observers that there is little musical tradition among the Sinhalese. He admits that there is no well-defined classical music and that the influence of India has been great, but points out that a large body of folk songs exists, that Kandyan dancers have always sung to the accompaniment of small cymbals, drums, pipes, and fiddles, and that the Sinhalese kings had bands of musicians, who used some seventy-five different musical instruments, including twenty-six varieties of wind instruments and eight kinds of *vina.* Surya Sena has been very active in reviving Sinhalese music, believing "that Lanka will find her soul through her own culture and music."

In the villages women seated in groups on the ground often play the *rabana,* a sort of community drum, beating out gay rhythms with their fingers, extemporizing songs as they play or singing folk tunes. One of the unusual experiences of visitors to rural Ceylon is to come unexpectedly upon *rabana* players, obviously enjoying their unique substitute for afternoon bridge.

Two imported song styles, one from Kaffir songs brought in by African mercenaries, and rhythmic *baila* tunes, from the Portuguese, which are sung to Sinhalese words, are still popular, even in the cities.

Dance

The Kandyan dance is a vital Sinhalese art form still practiced with undiminished vigor. It is what the distinguished Ceylonese painter, George Keyt, calls a "people's art," derived from classical sources, whose drummers, dancers, and teachers are from the peasant class, maintaining "one of the purest forms of national expression in Ceylon."

Some of the professional performers hold land from the temples in return for their occasional services, as their ancestors did under the Sinhalese kings. The dancers are all men, though a few women occasionally try the essentially masculine and athletic form. As they dance they sing songs descriptive of the movement of animals, rhythmically depicting the slow tread of an elephant or the gliding flight of a hawk that suddenly swoops upon its prey, or telling the ancient stories of Ceylon and Buddhism. There are several varieties of Kandyan dance, all originally associated with religious ceremonies. The sight of a well-trained troupe of Kandyan dancers, in their magnificent costumes, going through their routines to the beat of double-ended, keg-shaped drums, is one of the most exciting things that Ceylon can show.

The costume for the most spectacular of the Kandyan dances, the *Ves,* as described by Keyt, is worth recording: patterned silver plates which stand out around the forehead, from which hang little shining Bo-leaves of silver; mango-shaped sheaths covering the ears; a silver plate over the forehead and silver bands attached to the lacquered, bell-shaped crest on the top of the head; an ornamental silver throatlet; cobra-shaped sheaths over the arms near the shoulders; brightly colored open beadwork ornaments on the chest; bracelets and butterfly-shaped wristlets; a great ornamental girdle with tapering pendant, decorated with globular patterns; a white *dhoti,* covered at the top by a red cloth and five pleated, frilled strips hanging down around the waist; rattling anklets.

Not all Kandyan dancers are so gorgeously dressed,

207

for some of the variations require simpler costumes. Sometimes only the *dhoti* or lower garment is worn, with a turban; in others the waist is decorated with three frills, bordered with red.

The drummers play standing, following any one of a number of strictly prescribed patterns of classical rhythms. They have an amazingly wide range of pitch, varying tempos, staccato and sustained notes, playing with intense energy for hours at a time, striking with strong fingers both ends of the long drums, suspended from their waists. The beat is marked by other performers with small brass cymbals, and by the jingling anklets on the dancers.

In addition to the Kandyan dances, the Sinhalese have masked ceremonial dances. Some of these are associated with exorcism of evil spirits, which are thought to have produced illnesses. The manufacture of masks and the dancing, which has undoubtedly declined in modern years, are concentrated in the village of Ambalangoda, not far from Galle, on Ceylon's west coast. The masks are of various kinds, carved out of light wood and brightly painted. Some, worn by boys, represent dogs; others, with beaks, out of which crawl cobras, and wing-like ear-pieces, are peacock masks; others, with hooded cobras forming a kind of crown and cobras writhing in ear-pieces and dripping from the nostrils, with very white fangs in a bright red mouth, are *naga* or snake masks. Martin Wickramasinghe says that these masks are a "peculiar contribution of the Sinhalese culture which deserves more attention from artists and ethnologists."

Growing out of the devil dancing is a satirical masked folk dancing in which various types like soldiers, money-lenders, and butchers are caricatured with great cleverness. The masks, carved by peasant craftsmen, are vital, ribald, and forceful, but lack artistic distinction. A dramatic form called *Kolam,* using character masks and told in dance pantomine, accompanied by chanted verses and the inevitable drums, has developed from the earlier, crude folk dances. *Kolam* (which means "costume" or "representation") tells legendary stories involving mythological figures and stories based on village life, concerning policemen, soldiers, a herald, a *dhoby* (washerman), and a royal family, in all some sixty characters. The masks are marvelous pieces of craftsmanship, especially the tremendous, ornate masks of the king and queen (the king's crown is at least five feet high). It is worth a traveler's visit to Ambalangoda to see the *Kolam* masks and perhaps watch an evening of dancing. Cheap copies of some of these masks, of inferior workmanship, can be bought in the bazaars of Colombo.

Classical Indian dances have been kept alive by the Tamils and are very popular in Ceylon today, even among Sinhalese girls, who practice long hours to acquire the muscular control and the graceful, infinitely varied hand and finger movements of the Bharata Natya, which has 108 primary poses. The Manipuri style, from northeast India, gay, rhythmic, colorful popular dancing, is also greatly admired in Ceylon.

Drama

Perhaps because Hinayana Buddhism has little ritual out of which might grow a religious drama, there is almost no dramatic tradition in Ceylon. The *Kolam* plays are interesting, but hardly above the level of primitive folk drama. Puppet plays, using three-quarters lifesize figures, operated on the floor from low tables, using stock figures of Sinhalese kings and comic characters, no doubt imitated from the *Kolam* masks, are performed in southern Ceylon, but are of quite recent origin. Historical plays and pageants are sometimes performed, usually in celebration of religious events or on occasions of patriotic importance. A kind of folk opera, in which a "Presenter" tells the story in musical recitation, as actors represent the characters in song and dance, once popular along the west coast, now seems to be nearly extinct. Its place is taken by *Nurtiya,* an Indian form, with songs and music imitative of Indian musical shows.

The only study of Sinhalese drama has been made by E. R. Sarathchandra, who traces the origin of the various styles of popular drama to what he calls the folk religion of the village communities, influenced by rural beliefs and cults. He says that Sinhalese drama, music, and dance developed from this mixture of Buddhism and local beliefs and practices. On another plane, growing out of pure Buddhism, are the classical arts of painting, sculpture, architecture, and scholarly writing.

Under the British, some interest was aroused in Shakespeare and other Western playwrights, and ambitious amateurs have presented many classical and modern plays, mainly in Colombo. Several Ceylonese dramatists have written plays about Ceylon, but since there is no professional theatre, they have not had opportunities to master the craft of dramatic composition by giving it the test of first-class production. The enthusiasm is there, however, and Colombo even has an excellent theatre, which is part of the Lionel Wendt Cultural Center. In time, the Ceylonese, who are an instinctively dramatic and emotional people, will develop a national drama.

Literature

Martin Wickramasinghe, in his *Aspects of Sinhalese Culture*, says, "In art, architecture, and irrigation we have a past of which we can talk with genuine feeling. In literature we have a past which does not extend over seven hundred years and there is very little of it that can arouse enthusiasm." He blames the mediocrity of the so-called classical period of Sinhalese literature, from the tenth to the thirteenth century, on the influence of the decadent and superficial culture of India at that time. The absence of any evidence of literary achievement during what he calls "the flowering age of Sinhalese culture," from the fourth to the ninth century, however, is puzzling. It is possible, of course, that the books written during that time of artistic excellence, especially those with no religious significance that would not have been protected by Buddhist scholars, have been lost. It seems more likely that the Sinhalese genius, wonderfully expressed in stone and other real materials, found little outlet in literature. The fact that the language of scholarship was Pali and that Sinhalese was mainly a spoken language until about the tenth century is probably an important reason for the lack of literary tradition in Ceylon.

The Mahavamsa, written in Pali rather than in Sinhalese, remains the one important document of the ancient Sinhalese people, though its value today is historical rather than literary. Some very interesting non-religious poems, written on the stone wall of the gallery at Sigiriya between the eighth and tenth century, mostly in tribute to the maidens of the frescoes, indicate that poetry was a popular form of expression. The Sigiriya *Graffiti,* however, are hardly works of art, though quite revealing of Sinhalese men's frank admiration of physical beauty. Most visitors to Sigiriya today would fully sympathize with the anonymous poet who wrote on the wall below the frescoes such simple, forceful sentiments as

> Her lovely breasts
> Caused me to recall
> Swans drunk with nectar.

That there is real love of poetry among the Ceylonese today is evident from their numerous magazines and newspapers. Some of it is frankly imitative of Western poetry. A few young poets look back to the artificial patterns of classical Buddhist poetry or to the fifteenth century Sinhalese poets, Vattane and Vidagama, who broke with the Sanskrit influence from India and turned to simple themes of Buddhism and everyday life. Others seek inspiration in Sinhalese folk poetry, which has freshness and originality. One ardent nationalist, M. D. Ratnasuriya, has expressed the popular hope that "with cultural freedom, and extension of all cultural activities in a large variety of forms, the Sinhalese can produce a literature which can claim world recognition even in our time."

Early Sinhalese prose, for the most part repetitions of Indian stories, has no more claim to distinction than the poetry, though two thirteenth century writers, Gurulugomil and Dharmasena, are admired for their styles. The Sinhalese versions of the Buddhist *Jatakas,* tales of the various incarnations of Buddha, often as animals, have great charm and simplicity. The *Jatakas,* source of many of the folk tales of India which influenced Aesop and Kipling, have long been the subjects of temple decoration throughout Ceylon.

One of the results of European culture in Ceylon is the development of the Sinhalese novel, mainly a product of the twentieth century, though the form was known earlier. Written in Sinhalese, the novels were at first satirical attacks on the English-educated, privileged Ceylonese who were beginning to forget their own culture in adopting that of the English. Along with this element of class-consciousness is a sympathetic treatment of romantic love that may be one of the reasons for the low opinion in which the form is held by conservative Sinhalese, who are shocked at the idea of rebellion against family control of marriage. Among the few outstanding novelists are Piyadasa Sirisena and Martin Wickramasinghe.

* * * * *

The excellence of Ceylon's cultural achievements up to the twelfth century has never been approached since that time. The chaotic political and social conditions under the Indian conquerors, followed by the divisive influences of 450 years of colonialism, resulted in a lack of a coherent national point of view which has hampered the development of a distinctive modern Ceylonese culture. As the new country, now freed of European domination, goes through the difficult

process of assimilating its more or less insulated sepa-
rate groups into some semblance of unity, it will certainly begin to produce Ceylonese (rather than Sinhalese or Tamil or Moorish or Buddhist or Hindu or
Muslim or Christian) works of art. The people who
carved the Anuradhapura moonstones and built the
great *dagobas* and painted the Sigiriya ladies have in
them the instinct for beauty, dignity, and artistic form
that will again burst into great artistic expression.

8. *Some Sober Final Thoughts*

After the *apéritif* comes the dinner itself, nourishing and substantial. If the *hors d'oeuvres* have whetted your appetite for the rich feast of Ceylon, that is as it should be. You may now go to some of the books referred to in the bibliography that follows this chapter and enjoy the complete story of this wonderful country, of which this little book has given only a brief summary. Or, better still, you can travel by plane or ship to see for yourself the delights of Sri Lanka.

The picture is by no means complete. For example, much more might be said about the fine botanical gardens at Peradeniya and Hakgalle, whose avenues of royal palms, fern trees, and carefully tended beds of exotic flowers are of extraordinary interest; about the two National Parks, Ruhuna and Wilpattu, in whose nearly 300 square miles may be seen in their natural state the fascinating animals and birds of Ceylon; about the magic of the jungle, so beautifully described by John Still in *Jungle Tide,* inexorably creeping in to cover the transient works of man; about the endless delights of highland Ceylon, whose beauty and variety should be shouted abroad to attract leisurely lovers of natural splendor, not simply those with thirty-six hours before their ship leaves, during which a tourist agency arranges to have them get a tantalizing glimpse of Kandy and Nuwara Eliya. The statistics about schools and tea production are essential, but too impersonal and uncolorful. Ceylon is a very personal and colorful country which loses a great deal in a black and white picture such as this book necessarily gives.

There might be more about the people of Ceylon, not as sociological phenomena with castes and high birth-rate and political and economic problems, but as sweet, friendly individuals who happily dig holes in paved streets for the pillars of *pandals,* the decorative arches that welcome distinguished visitors; who fly kites fashioned like gaudy oriental butterflies; who squat gossiping in the middle of the road oblivious to traffic or who, behind the wheel of an automobile, use their horns with joyous abandon; who love nothing in the world better than a *tamasha,* any kind of celebration, regardless of its reason for being; who, if they hear the cry of a gecko, the dainty, transparent house-lizard of Ceylon, consider it a warning which may keep the more superstitious home that day; who laugh often and love flowers and children and holidays; whose friendly greetings, "ayubowen" (Sinhalese) and "nam-askaram" (Tamil), said with the hands together as in prayer, are genuinely hospitable and kind.

There should be more about the loveliness of the country: an outrigger canoe with tawny sail coming out of the sunset; a flame tree in bloom in March, like a great torch among the coconut palms; the temple trees, their blooms ivory white in the twilight, perfuming the air with a scent reminiscent of gardenias; the patterns of color across the ridges of dry paddy fields as the women of Jaffna walk to a well for water, carrying their brass and pottery jars on their heads; the lagoon of Batticaloa on a moonlit night as the singing fish send up their thin wail; the weird woodland of Horton Plains, its patches of forest among the *patanas* hung with Spanish moss; a tiny white *dagoba* up-country, upon which the parapet of mountains looks protectively, holding out of the Uva Valley the banks of fog that threaten the passes; the heaps of bright orange king coconuts, pineapples, and unroasted *cadju* nuts in a village on the road to Kandy; the creak of a two-wheeled *cadjan*-canopied cart, pulled by a tiny, humped bullock, his hide scrawled with cabalistic marks; fishermen standing on the steps of fixed stilts beyond a sandy beach, their slender, strong bodies silhouetted against the sky; a line of paddy-field workers, naked except for loin-cloths, swinging in unison the big hoes called *mammoties,* chanting as they move forward, as in a folk ballet; a catamaran, its sail lowered, coming onto a Jaffna beach from the blue Bay of Bengal; a flotilla of fishing boats hurrying in before a storm at Dondra Head; an elephant bathing in the Mahaveli-ganga.

There could be more about the extraordinary things that are peculiar to Ceylon: the octagonal library above the crenellated moat of the Temple of the Tooth in Kandy; a serviceable sluice in the channel from an artificial lake, built two thousand years ago; an exquisite, lotus-shaped ancient bath, near a leaning granite pillar on which sits a big gray monkey; the annual "pilgrimage" of millions of butterflies to Adam's Peak; the round silver trays etched by the craftsmen of Kandy with the figures of moonstones; the medieval Passion Play, on wagons, complete with Roman soldiers, performed on Good Friday in a coastal village near Negombo; stars emerging from rough stones ground by lapidaries who turn their wheels with hand-bows; the great tangle of needles and thread on the trail to Adam's Peak, left by generations of pilgrims at the place where Lord Buddha is said to have stopped to sew up a tear in his robe.

Perhaps more should be said about the menacing

things: the precarious economy that may not be able to cope with the rising population, the fluctuating demand for Ceylon's tea and rubber, and the dependence of the country on a favorable trade balance to buy the food it does not produce; the sinister communal rivalry; the fear and hatred and unhappiness where there should be trust and love and beauty; the growing strength of communism, whose principles, hidden under popular causes, nourished by poverty and injustice and dissatisfaction, are alien to the beliefs of all the great faiths represented in Ceylon.

If this short book arouses curiosity about the grace and charm of this fair island, however, it will have accomplished its purpose. If it sometimes seems to picture an Eden into which the serpent has crept, the emphasis is on Eden, the blessed garden, not on the serpent of social and political unrest. Sri Lanka—so beautiful, so fruitful, so hallowed, so long-enduring, so hopeful, so naturally gifted with an understanding of freedom—deserves a bright future. May Ceylon resolve her difficulties under the national flag whose golden lion and stripes symbolize the union of all her people, so that once more "the resplendent land" may have peace.

Bibliography

BOOKS

ARIYAPALA, M. B. *Society in Medieval Ceylon.* Colombo: K. V. G. de Silva, 1956.

Art and Architecture of Ceylon, Polonnaruva Period. Bombay: Arts Council of Ceylon, 1954.

BAILEY, SYDNEY D. *Ceylon.* London: Hutchinson's Library, 1952.

BOLTIN, LEE. *Ceylon.* Garden City, N. Y.: Nelson Doubleday, Inc., 1956.

BROHIER, R. *Ancient Irrigation Works in Ceylon.* 3 vols. Colombo: Ceylon Government Press, 1934–35, 1949–50.

BURTON, RICHARD F. *The Book of the Thousand Nights and a Night: A Plain and Literal Translation of the Arabian Nights Entertainments.* 6 vols. (bound into 3 books) New York: The Heritage Press, 1934.

CAVE, HENRY W. *The Book of Ceylon.* London: Cassell and Co., 1908.

———. *Ruined Cities of Ceylon.* London: Cassell and Co., 1897.

Ceylon, A Tourist Guide. Colombo: Government Tourist Bureau, 1951.

Ceylon—1957. Department of State Publication 6474, June, 1957.

Ceylon Paintings from Temple, Shrine, and Rock. Preface by W. G. Archer, Introduction by S. Paranavitana. New York Graphic Society, by arrangement with UNESCO, 1957.

Ceylon Year Book. Colombo: Department of Census and Statistics. (appears annually)

CLARKE, ARTHUR C. *The Reefs of Taprobane, Underwater Adventures Around Ceylon*. London: Frederick Muller, Ltd., 1957.

CODRINGTON, H. W. *A Short History of Ceylon*. London: Macmillan and Co., 1947.

COLLINS, SIR CHARLES HENRY. *Public Administration in Ceylon*. London, New York: Royal Institute of International Affairs, 1951.

COOK, ELSIE K. and K. KULARATNAM. *Ceylon, Its Geography, Its Resources and Its People*. London: Macmillan and Co., 1951.

COOMARASWAMY, ANANDA. *Medieval Sinhalese Art*. Broad Campden: Essex House Press, 1908.

———. *The Dance of Shiva*. New York: Noonday Press, 1957.

CROWE, PHILIP. *Diversions of a Diplomat in Ceylon*. New York: D. Van Nostrand, 1956.

Economic Development of Ceylon. Report of a Mission Organized by the International Bank for Reconstruction and Development at the Request of the Government of Ceylon. Baltimore: Johns Hopkins Press, 1953.

ELIOT, SIR CHARLES N. E. *Hinduism and Buddhism*. 3 vols. London: E. Arnold and Co., 1912.

FARQUHAR, J. N. *A Primer of Hinduism*. New York: Oxford, 1912.

Ferguson's Ceylon Directory. Colombo: The Ceylon Observer. (appears annually)

GEIGER, WILHELM, trans. *The Culavamsa, Being the More Recent Part of the Mahavamsa*. 2 vols. Colombo: Ceylon Government Information Department, 1953.

————. *The Mahavamsa, or The Great Chronicle of Ceylon.* Colombo: Ceylon Government Information Department, 1950.

GIBB, H. A. R. *Mohammedanism, An Historical Survey.* New York: Mentor Books, 1955.

GODAKUMBURA, C. E. *Sinhalese Literature.* Colombo: The Colombo Apothecaries' Co., Ltd., 1955.

HULUGALLE, H. A. J. *Introducing Ceylon.* Colombo: Ceylon Government Department of Information, 1949.

HUMPHREYS, CHRISTMAS. *Buddhism.* Hammondworth: Penguin Books, 1951.

JAYAWARDENE, M. D. H. *Economic and Social Development of Ceylon—A Survey,* 1926–54. The Ministry of Finance, 1955.

JENNINGS, SIR IVOR. *The Constitution of Ceylon.* London: Oxford University Press, 1953.

————. *The Economy of Ceylon.* London: Oxford University Press, 1948.

———— and N. W. TAMBIAH. *The Dominion of Ceylon: The Development of its Laws and Constitution.* London: Stevens and Sons, Ltd., 1952.

KEBLE, W. T. *Ceylon Beaten Track.* Colombo: Lake House, 1951.

KOTELAWALA, SIR JOHN. *An Asian Prime Minister's Story.* London: George G. Harrap and Co., 1956.

LAW, BIMALA CHURN. *On the Chronicles of Ceylon.* Calcutta: Royal Asiatic Society of Bengal, 1947.

LUDOWYK, E. F. C. (ed.). *Robert Knox in the Kandyan Kingdom.* London: Oxford University Press, 1948.

LUSHINGTON, CICELY. *Bird Life in Ceylon.* Colombo: Times of Ceylon, n.d.

MENDIS, GARRETT C. *Ceylon Under the British.* Colombo: Colombo Apothecaries' Co., Ltd., 1948.

223

————. *The Early History of Ceylon.* Calcutta: Y.M.C.A. Publishing House, 1948. 5th ed.

————. *Ceylon Today and Yesterday,* "Main Currents of Ceylon History," Colombo: Lake House, 1957.

MURRAY, JOHN. *A Handbook for Travellers in India, Pakistan, Ceylon.* 17th ed. London: John Murray, 1955.

NAMASIVAYAM, SAGARAJASINGHAM. *The Legislatures of Ceylon, 1928–48.* London: Faber and Faber, 1951.

NEILL, STEPHEN CHARLES. *Under Three Flags.* New York: Friendship Press, 1954.

NICHOLAS, S. E. N. *Fascinating Ceylon.* Colombo: Times, 1950.

OLDENBERG, H. ed. and translator. *Dīpavaṃsa.* London: 1879.

Oxford Economic Atlas for India and Ceylon. Oxford University Press, 1953.

PARANAVITANA, S. *Guide to Polonnaruwa.* Colombo: Ceylon Government Press, 1950.

————. *The Stupa in Ceylon.* Colombo: 1946.

PARKER, A. *Ancient Ceylon.* London: 1909.

PERERA, G. F. *The Ceylon Railway.* Colombo: 1925.

PERERA, L. H. HORACE. *Ceylon Under Western Rule.* Madras: Macmillan, 1955.

PIERIS, RALPH. *Sinhalese Social Organization, The Kandyan Period.* Colombo: Ceylon University Press, 1956.

PURCHAS, SAMUEL. *Hakluytus Posthumus or Purchas His Pilgrimes.* 20 vols. Glasgow: James MacLehose and Sons, 1906.

————. *Purchas His Pilgrimage.* 5 vols. London: Wm. Sansby for Henrie Fetherstone, 1614.

RHYS DAVIDS, T. W. *Buddhism, Its History and Literature.* 3rd ed. New York: 1918.

RYAN, BRYCE. *Caste in Modern Ceylon.* New Brunswick: Rutgers University Press, 1953.

SARATHCHANDRA, E. R. *The Sinhalese Folk Play.* Colombo: The Ceylon University Press, 1953.

————. *The Sinhalese Novel.* Colombo: M. D. Gunasena Co., 1950.

SARKAR, N. K. *Population Problems and Aspects of Economic Development of Ceylon.* Cambridge: 1956.

SELIGMAN, C. G. and B. Z. *Veddas.* Cambridge: 1911.

SENEVERATNA, JOHN M. *Dutugemenu, His Life and Times.* Colombo: Sinha Publications, 1946.

————. *Sri Pada.* Colombo: Ceylon Daily News, n.d.

SPITTEL, RICHARD. *Wild Ceylon.* Colombo: Colombo Book Center, 1924.

————. *Savage Sanctuary.* Colombo: Colombo Book Center, 1941.

STILL, JOHN. *The Jungle Tide.* London: William Blackwood and Sons, 1930.

TENNENT, SIR JAMES EMERSON. *Ceylon, An Account of the Island, Physical, Historical and Topographical.* 2 vols. 3rd ed. London: Longman, Green, Longman and Roberts, 1950.

The Colombo Plan for Cooperative Economic Development in South and South-East Asia. Commonwealth Consultative Committee on South and South-East Asia. Colombo: Ceylon Government Press, 1950.

THOMAS, E. J. *The Life of Buddha as Legend and History.* London: 1927, 1930.

THOMAS, P. *Hindu Religion, Customs and Manners.* Bombay: D. P. Taraporevala Sons and Co., Ltd., n.d.

VIJAYATUNGA, J. *Island Story.* Madras: Oxford University Press, 1949.

225

VITTACHI, TARZIE. *Emergency '58: The Story of the Ceylon Race Riots*. London: Andre Deutsch, 1958

WEERAWARDANA, I. D. S. and MARGUERITE WEERAWARDANA. *Ceylon and Her Citizens*. London: Oxford University Press, 1956.

WICKRAMASINGHE, MARTIN. *Aspects of Sinhalese Culture*. Mount Lavinia: Mount Press, n.d.

———. *Sinhalese Literature*. Trans. by E. R. Sarathchandra. Colombo: M. D. Gunasena Co., 1949.

WIJESEKERA, N. D. *The People of Ceylon*. Colombo: M. D. Gunasena and Co., Ltd., 1949.

WILLIAMS, HARRY. *Ceylon, Pearl of the East*. London: Robert Hale, Ltd., 1950.

WIRZ, PAUL. *Exorcism and the Art of Healing in Ceylon*. Leiden: E. J. Brill, 1954.

WOOLF, LEONARD. *Village in the Jungle*. New Phoenix Library. London: Chatto and Windus, 1951.

ARTICLES

BARNETT, L. D. "The Early History of Ceylon," *Cambridge History of India*. Vol. I, Chap. XXV. Cambridge: 1922.

"Basic Data on the Economy of Ceylon," *World Trade Information Service Economic Reports,* Part I, No. 57–75. Washington, D. C.: U. S. Department of Commerce, 1957.

BROHIER, R. L. "Ceylon-Dutch Domestic Art," *Kalamanjari,* I, no. 1 (1950).

"Ceylon," *Fact Sheets on the Commonwealth,* No. R 2790. London: Reference Division, Central Office of Information, June, 1956.

BIBLIOGRAPHY

CHRISTIANS, WILLIAM F. and G. P. MALALASEKERA. "The Dominion of Ceylon," Chap. XV of *India, Pakistan, Ceylon,* edited by W. Norman Brown. Ithaca: Cornell University Press, 1951.

CRANE, ROBERT I. *Aspects of Economic Development in South Asia,* with a Supplement on "Development Problems in Ceylon" by Burton Stein. New York: Institute of Pacific Relations, International Secretariat, 1954.

CUMARASWAMY, A. M. K. "Hinduism in Ceylon," *Pageant of Lanka.* Colombo: 1948.

HOCART, A. M. "Archaeology," an appendix to H. W. Codrington's *Short History of Ceylon.* (see above)

HULTZSCH, E. "Contributions to Singhalese Chronology," *Journal of the Royal Asiatic Society of Great Britain* (1913).

KEYT, GEORGE. "Kandyan Dancing," *Times of Ceylon Annual,* 1953.

LADEJINSKY, W. I. "Agriculture in Ceylon," *Foreign Agriculture,* (January, 1944).

MALALASEKERA, G. P. "Lanka's Contribution to Buddhist Culture," *Pageant of Lanka.* Colombo: 1948.

MENDIS, GARRETT C. "Ceylon," Parts 1 and 2, Chaps. XVIII and XIX of *A Comprehensive History of India,* Vol. 2, ed. by K. A. Nilakanta Sastri. Bombay: 1957.

MENDIS, J. C. "The Pali Chronicles of Ceylon," *University of Ceylon Review,* IV.

———. "The Chronology of the Early Pali Chronicles of Ceylon," *University of Ceylon Review,* V.

PARANAVITANA, S. "Mahayanism in Ceylon," *Ceylon Journal of Science,* II.

———. "Pre-Buddhist Religious Beliefs in Ceylon," *Journal of the Ceylon Branch of the Royal Asiatic Society,* XXXI.

227

RATNASURIYA, M. D. "The Evolution of Sinhalese Language and Literature," *Pageant of Lanka*. Colombo: 1948.

RUSSELL, MARTIN. "The '43 Group's Tenth Anniversary," *Times of Ceylon Annual,* 1953.

SARATHCHANDRA, E. R. "Kolam, the Life Art of Caricature," *Times of Ceylon Annual,* 1954.

SURYA SENA, DEVAR. "Sinhalese Music," *Pageant of Lanka*. Colombo: 1948.

VANKATARAMAN, K. S. "Indian Music," *Kalamanjari,* I, no. 1 (1950).

Glossary

BAHIRAVAYAS—The gay, dancing, singing, instrument-playing dwarfs of early Sinhalese sculpture.

BAILA—Popular rhythmic melodies, with Portuguese influence.

BANIYAN—A kind of singlet or short-sleeved jersey.

BHIKKU—A saffron-robed, shaven-headed Buddhist monk, who usually carries a palm-leaf fan, a black umbrella, and, sometimes, a begging bowl.

BRAHMAN—The Hindu caste of priests.

BURGHER—A descendant of Dutch and other European employees of the Dutch East India Company.

BURIANI—A popular Ceylonese dish made of rice, mutton, and spices.

CADJAN—Palm-leaves, used for roofs and fences, and for the canopies of bullock-carts.

CADJU—The cashew nut.

CAMBOY—A sarong-like skirt, worn with a bodice by some Ceylonese women.

CHANK—A Sinhalese horn made from a seashell.

CHENA—A kind of marginal farming in jungle clearings.

CONDE—Long hair rolled into a knot, like a chignon, worn by some elderly Sinhalese men, and, generally, by women.

Culavamsa—"Lesser Dynasty," a continuation of *The Mahavamsa.*

DAGOBA—The typical bell-shaped, spired Buddhist shrine of Ceylon, always painted white. In size dagobas range from structures as big as the Pyramids to small village shrines not more than twelve feet high.

DALADA MALIGAWA—The Temple of the Tooth, in which is enshrined the sacred tooth of Buddha.

229

DHOBY—Washerman.

DHOTI—An Indian garment covering the lower body, worn by men. It differs from the sarong in having one end passing between the legs, diaper-fashion.

DURAVA—The Sinhalese "toddy-tapper" caste.

GANSABHAS—Village Councils.

GE—A broad Sinhalese family group, bearing a distinctive name.

GHEE—Buffalo-milk butter.

GINGELLY—Sesame.

GOYIGAMA—The Sinhalese "cultivator" caste.

JAK—A large tree, bearing edible fruit weighing as much as forty pounds each. The yellow-colored wood is valuable in making furniture, etc.

JATAKAS—Tales of the incarnations of Buddha.

KABRAGOYA—The big monitor lizard of Ceylon.

KARAVA—The Sinhalese "fisher" caste.

KARMA—The influence on future existence of one's deeds in this life, part of both Buddhist and Hindu belief.

KRAAL—Elephant round-up, for capture of wild elephants, discontinued in 1951.

KSHATRIYAS—The Hindu king and warrior caste.

KURAKKAN—A barley-like cereal.

KURAVAN—Telegu-speaking gypsies.

LAMPRIES—Rice and curry wrapped in plantain leaves.

LANKA SAMA SAMAJA PARTY (LSSP)—"Ceylon Equality Party," a Trotskyite Marxist political party.

MAHAJANA EKSATH PERAMUNA (MEP)—"People's United Front," a coalition of several political parties which gained power in 1956.

MAHAVAMSA—The epic poem of Buddhism in Ceylon, written in Pali under the editorship of a monk named Mahanama in the fourth century A.D. The name means "Great Dynasty." It covers the period from Vijaya to 352 A.D.

MAMMOTIES—Heavy-headed hoes.

MOUILLE—A popular dish of fish and rice.

MUDALI—An aristocratic Goyigama subcaste.

NAGAS—A primitive pre-historic Ceylonese tribe of snake worshipers. The word "naga" means snake.

NAGASVARA—An Indian clarinet.

OLA—A manuscript made of incised talipot palm leaves, bound between board covers.

PANCHAMAS—Hindu outcastes.

PANDAL—A decorative arch.

PANTHERU—A tambourine.

PATANAS—Rolling, treeless grassland of the up-country plains.

PERAHERA—A ceremonial parade.

PILAU—A popular rice dish.

PIRIVENA—A school for the training of Buddhist *bhikkus.*

PONGI—An Indian wind instrument.

RABANA—A Sinhalese community drum.

RADALA—A Goyigama subcaste of Kandyan aristocrats.

RAGAS—Basic combinations of sound in Karnatic music.

RAKSHAS—See YAKKHAS.

RILAWA—A species of small monkey.

RODIYA—Sinhalese outcaste beggars.

SALAGAMA—The Sinhalese "cinnamon-peeler" caste.

SAMBHUR—The Ceylon elk.

SAMBOL—Relishes, which may be highly spiced, eaten with curries.

SANGHA—The monastic order of Buddhist *bhikkus,* the Buddhist clergy.

SARANGI—A violin-like Indian musical instrument.

231

SAREE—The typical female dress of India and Ceylon, six or seven yards of cloth, about forty-five inches wide, usually draped over blouses.

SARONG—Skirt-like covering of the lower body, lengths of cloth, twisted at the waist, worn by Ceylonese men.

SATYAGRAHA—A form of Gandhian "civil disobedience."

SHERWANI—A dress costume, worn by some (usually well-to-do) men of India and Ceylon, mid-thigh length black or white jackets, buttoned from hem to throat.

SITAR—An Indian stringed musical instrument.

SRI PADA—Adam's Peak, literally "the sacred footprint," one of the high mountain peaks of Ceylon.

STUPA—Same as *dagoba.*

SUDRAS—The Hindu laborer caste.

SWABHASHA—The indigenous languages of Ceylon, Sinhalese and Tamil.

TALAGOYA—The iguana.

TAMASHA—A celebration or party.

TIC POLONGA—The Russell's viper, a vicious poisonous snake.

VAISYAS—The Hindu merchant and farmer caste.

VEDDAHS—An aboriginal cave-dwelling tribe of eastern Ceylon, now nearly extinct.

VES—A spectacular Kandyan dance.

VIHARA—A Buddhist monastery.

VINA—An Indian musical instrument.

VIPLAVAKARI LANKA SAMA SAMAJA PARTY (VLSSP)—"Revolutionary Ceylon Equality Party," a Marxist political party.

WANDEROO—The gray ape of Ceylon.

YAKKHAS—A primitive pre-historic Ceylonese tribe of demon-worshipers.

Index

Adam's Bridge, 63–64
Adam's Peak (Sri Pada), 9, 176–179, 219
Afghans, 36
Agriculture, 138–148
Ajanta Caves, 201
Alexander the Great, 3, 6, 9
Anuradhapura, 74–75
Aquinas University, 59
Arabian Nights, 8, 12–13
Arabs, 8, 11, 35
Architecture, 192–196
Arunachalam, Sir Ponnamba-lam, 111
Asoka, 70, 72, 199
Astrology, 51

Bahiravayas, 198
Bailey, Rev. Benjamin, 14
Baluchis, 36
Bandaranaike, S. W. R. D., 115–118, 126, 127, 128
Bandung Conference, 128
Banking, 158–160
Bengal, Bay of, 1, 28
Birds, 27–28
Borahs, 36
Bo-tree, 72–73, 78
Brahmans, 40, 46
British East India Company, 104–105
British Period, 104–114

Buddha, Gautama, 10, 11, 67, 98, 171, 172, 219
Buddhism, 10–11, 30, 70–74, 172–181, 191, 210
Hinayana, 173
Mahayana, 173
Burghers, 37–38, 103
Burton, Sir Richard, 4

Caine, Sir Sydney, 139
Caste Systems, 40–47
Catholicism, 99
Ceylon,
area, 18
central government, 119–126
cabinet, 120–121
judiciary, 122–125
local government, 125–126
parliament, 121–122
climate, 21–22
description, 16–29
distances to other parts of the world, 19
fauna, 24–29
history, 62–118
independence, 114–118
location, 1–2, 18
mean temperature and hu-midity, 18
names, 3–5
people, 29–53
principal mountain peaks, 18

principal rivers, 18
rainfall, 19
size, 2
topography, 19–21
vegetation, 22–24
Ceylon National Congress, 110
Ceylon Technical College, 59
Ceylonization, 142, 162
Cheras, 32
China, 9, 10, 38, 93–94
China (People's Republic), 134–135, 144–145
Cholas, 32, 83, 88–89, 93
Christianity, 37, 185–186
Class distinctions, 47–49
Clarke, Arthur C., 28
Clothing, 53–54
Cobras, 171
Coconuts, 136, 145–148
Codrington, H. W., 99
Colebrooke Reforms, 108–109
Colombo, 17
Colombo Plan, 12, 128, 134, 164
Commercial policy, 162
Communications, 157–158
Communism, 134–135
Communist Party, 130, 131
Coomaraswamy, Ananda, 199, 200, 201, 203, 205
Culavamsa, 66, 73–74, 90–91
Cumaraswamy, A. M. K., 181, 182

Dagobas, 73–75, 87, 192–196, 215
  Abyayagiri, 193
  Ambastala, 72

Ruanweli, 194
Thuperama, 193
Dahanayake, Wijayananda, 118
Dambulla, 83, 191, 202
Dance, 206–210
De Almeida, Dom Lourenço, 94–95
Deepavali Festival, 184, 186
Deraniyagala, Justin, 203
Development Programs, 163–165
Devil-dancing, 171, 208–209
Dipavamsa, 66, 74
Divorce, 51–52
Dondra Head, 18, 219
Donoughmore Commission, 112–113
Dutch East India Company, 37, 101, 107
Dutch occupation, 100–103
Dutch Reformed Church, 102
Drama, 210–211
Durava, 43–45
Dutthagamini, 25, 74–83, 84, 193, 194, 202

Education, 55–61
Elara, 76–82, 202
Elephants, 24–25
Esala Perahera, 97, 179–181
Eurasians, 38
Europeans, 38
Exter, John, 159

Family unit, 49–53
Fish, 28–29
Flowers, 23
Food, 54–55

Gampaha, 24, 94
Ge names, 49
Gems, 21, 151–152
Goanese, 38
Goonetilleke, Sir Oliver, 114, 117, 119
Goyigama, 43–45, 47
Gross National Product, 167
Gunawardene, R. S. S., 134

Hakgalle Botanical Garden, 24, 216
Henaratgoda Botanical Gardens, 143
Hinduism, 181–185
Hindus, 32, 34
Horton Plains, 20, 218

Ibn Batuta, 8–9, 11, 177
India, 1, 22, 23, 30, 34, 65, 133
Industry, 148–151
International Bank Mission, 139, 142, 144, 147, 150, 163, 165, 166
International Cooperation Administration (ICA), 12, 165
Irrigation Tanks, 87–88, 90, 92–93

Jaffna, 1, 16, 17, 19, 24, 35, 92–93
Jaffna College, 59, 186
Jatakas, Buddhist, 213–214
Jennings, Sir Ivor, 113

Kaffirs, 38
Kandula, 80–82
Kandyan Dancing, 188, 206–208
Karava, 43–44

Kasyapa, King, 83–87, 201, 202
Kataragama, 64, 183–184
Kelaniya, 77
Keyt, George, 188, 203, 206, 207
Knox, Robert, 40, 101
Kolam masks, 189, 209, 210
Kotelawala, Sir John, 111, 115, 128, 129, 144–145, 177
Kotte Dynasty, 94, 96
Kshatrias, 43, 46
Kublai Khan, 11
Kuravans, 39
Kurunegala, 86

Labor and employment, 165–167
Languages, 33–34, 60–61
Lanka Sama Samaja Party (LSSP), 127, 128, 130, 131, 132, 133, 166
Legends, 62–66
Lionel Wendt Cultural Center, 211
Literacy, 56
Literature, 211, 214
Lizards, 10, 26
Loris, 26

Mahajana Eksath Peramuna (MEP), 115, 126, 129–131
Mahanama, 84
Mahavamsa, 66–83, 84, 200, 212
Mahinda, 70–72, 172
Malalasekera, G. P., 190–191
Malays, 36
Maldive Islands, 2
Marco Polo, 2, 11, 177

Marriage, 50–52
Masks, 208–209
Mendis, G. C., 107–108
Mihintale, 71–72
Milton, John, 3, 5, 6
Minerals, 21, 151–153
Mining, 151–153
Monsoons, 21–22
Moonstones, 197–198, 215
Moore, Sir Henry, 114
Moors, 35–37, 95–96
Music, 203–206
Muslims, 36, 185

Names, 40
Nestorian Catholics, 7
North, Honorable Frederick, 105
Nuwara Eliya, 64
Nuwara Eliya Plains, 20

Ovid, 5

Painting, 199–203
Palk Strait, 1, 63
Panchamas, 46
Pandyans, 32, 93
Parakrama Bahu the Great, 83, 89–92, 196, 198, 199
Paranavitana, Senarat, 200, 201
Parsees, 38
Patanas, 24, 218
Pegu, 89, 93
Peradeniya Gardens, 24, 216
Peraheras, 25
Perera, G. F., 157
Perera, Dr. N. M., 127, 128, 132, 133, 166
Pieris, Harry, 203

Pliny, 2, 6, 9
Political parties, 126–131
    problems, 132–135
Polonnaruwa, 88–93
Population, 29–30, 137
Portuguese Occupation, 94–99
Power, 153–154
Ptolemy, 4, 6–7
Purchas, Samual, 13–14
Purdah, 36

Racial distinctions, 39–40
    organization, 30
Rajasinha I, 96–97
Rajasinha II, 100–101
Rajasinha, Sri Wickrama, 66, 105
Ramanathan, Sir Ponnambalam, 111
Ramayana, 4, 62–64
Ratnapura, 21
Ratnasuriya, M. D., 213
Religion, 170–187
Rodiyas, 43–44
Roman-Dutch Code of Laws, 31, 102, 124
Rubber, 136, 137, 143–145
Rubber-Rice Trade Agreement of 1952, 134, 144–145
Ruhuna National Park, 27, 217
Ryan, Bryce, 41–43, 46

Salagama, 43–45
Sanghamitta, 72
Sarathchandra, E. R., 210
School attendance, 57
Sculpture, 196–199
Senanayake, Don Stephen, 111, 113, 114–115, 126, 128

Senanayake, Dudley, 115
Serendib, 4–5
Sigiriya, 83–86, 88, 202, 212
Sigiriya Frescoes, 83, 86, 189,
    191, 200–202, 215
Sindbad the Sailor, 2, 8, 13
Sinhalese, 30–32, 52–53
Sirisena, Piyadasa, 214
Snakes, 26–27, 171
Sopater, 7, 11
Soulbury, Lord, 113, 114
Spittel, Dr. Richard, 38
Sri Lanka Freedom Party, 115,
    118, 127
Stein, Burton, 168
Still, John, 217
Sudras, 46
Surya Sena, Devar, 205–206
Swabhasha, 33–34, 60

Tambiah, H. W., 113
Tamil Federal Party, 130, 131
Tamils, 32–35, 52–53
Taprobane, 3, 6, 7
Tea, 136, 137, 140–143
Temple of the Tooth (*Dalada
    Maligawa*), 25, 91, 98,
    180, 219
Tennent, Sir Emerson, 3, 5, 6,
    9, 10, 91, 95, 103, 106,
    204–205
Tissa, King Devanampiya, 70–
    72, 172, 193
Tooth Relic, 25, 93, 97–98,
    179–180
Tourism, 153

Trade, 160–161
Transportation, 154–157
Trincomalee, 20, 65, 104

UNESCO, 12, 56
United National Party, 114–
    115, 126–131
United Nations, 133–134, 164
University of Ceylon, 46, 58–59
University of London, 59

Vaisyas, 46
Veddahs, 10, 12, 38, 65
Vel Festival, 184, 186
Vidyalankara University, 59
Vidyodaya University, 60
Vijaya, 3, 4, 65–70, 171, 172,
    176, 202
Vijayatunga, J., 14–15
Viplavakari Lanka Sama Sa-
    maja Party (VLSSP), 127–
    128, 130
Vittachi, Tarzie, 116
Voice of America, 158

Walpole, Horace, 4
Wickramasinghe, Martin, 190,
    208–209, 211–212, 214
Wijesekera, Dr. N. D., 31, 32,
    36
Williams, Harry, 3, 38, 88, 102,
    146
Wilpattu National Park, 27,
    217
Woolf, Leonard, 183